Spheres

of

Love

spheres

TOWARD A NEW ETHICS

OF THE FAMILY

Love

STEPHEN · G · POST

Southern Methodist University Press
Dallas

Requests for permission to reproduce material
from this work should be sent to:
Rights and Permissions
Southern Methodist University Press
Box 415
Dallas, Texas 75275

LIBRARY OF CONGRESS CATALOGING-IN-PUBLICATION DATA

Post, Stephen Garrard, 1951–
    Spheres of love : toward a new ethics of the family / Stephen G. Post. —
1st ed.
      p.   cm.
    Includes bibliographical references and index.
    ISBN 0–87074–370–8 — ISBN 0–87074–371–6 (pbk.)
    1. Family—Moral and ethical aspects. 2. Love—Moral and ethical aspects.
3. Love—religious aspects—Christianity. 4. Family—United States.
5. Family—Religious life. I. Title.
HQ518.P676   1994
306.85—dc20   94–7166

Cover photograph by Glenn Whitehead
Design by Barbara Whitehead

Printed in the United States of America
on acid-free paper
2 4 6 8 9 7 5 3 1

For Rev. William D. Eddy
(1924–1989)

Contents

Acknowledgments *ix*

Chapters

1. Introduction: Love Familial and Universal *1*
2. Married Love *17*
3. The Misuse of Sexual Love *35*
4. Parental Love *51*
5. Filial Love *71*
6. Familial Love: Self–Denial and Self-Concern *91*
7. Love for Strangers *109*
8. An Order of Love: Close Ties and Strangers *129*

Notes *147*
Selected Bibliography *165*
Index *169*

Acknowledgments

Tнıs воок is the product of five years of thinking and writing. But it is also the product of my theological and philosophical reflections on love that began in the early 1980s while a graduate student in ethics at the University of Chicago Divinity School, continued while on the humanities faculty at Marymount College in Tarrytown, New York, and came to some further fruition here at Case Western Reserve University.

Since my primary tasks over the last six years have been in the School of Medicine in the field of Biomedical Ethics, this book was written in the evening hours with the support of my wife Mitsuko and my daughter Emma, whom I thank deeply. Some of my ideas emerged after casual conversation with parents at the Fernway School playground in Shaker Heights, Ohio. So *Spheres of Love* is in part the creation of a neighborhood of families trying to make evening sense of the chaos of modern culture, and I thank my neighbors. Since parts of the book pertain to Biomedical Ethics, I wish to express appreciation to the stimulating environment of the Center for Biomedical Ethics of the School of Medicine.

Robert G. Leisey, Ph.D., an old friend and a philosopher by training, made his typically excellent editorial comments along the way. Professor Lonnie D. Kliever of Southern Methodist University kindly consented to review the manuscript after initial revisions. His comments were invaluable. Looking back a little further, I am grateful as well to the late Rev. William D. Eddy of Christ Episcopal Church in Tarrytown, for we often discussed the need for an ethics of the family as a community.

Finally, my appreciation to my parents, Henry and Marguerite Post, who like all good parents do the best they can.

GRATEFUL ACKNOWLEDGMENT is made to the editors and publishers of the following journals for permission to publish those portions of this book that are revisions of previously published articles: Chapter 3 is a thorough revision of "Love, Religion, and the Sexual Revolution," *Journal of Religion,* Vol. 72, No. 3, July 1992, 403–416; Chapter 7 is a thorough revision of "Conditional and Unconditional Love," *Modern Theology,* Vol. 7, No. 5, October 1991, 435–446; and Chapter 8 is a thorough revision of "Love and the Order of Beneficence," *Soundings: An Interdisciplinary Journal,* Vol. 75, No. 4, Winter 1992, 499–516.

Spheres
of
Love

1

Introduction:
Love Familial
and
Universal

My purpose is to discuss the importance of love in special relations, especially of marriage and of familial ties on the parent-child axis interpreted in the light of the often acrimonious American debate over "family values." My approach interweaves theological and philosophical ethics with cultural history. A second purpose is to consider how love for those near and dear can be rightly balanced with love for the stranger—the neighbor who is everyone and anyone. The concern with moral balance between love in the sphere of ongoing special relations of proximity, such as parental love, and love in the sphere of strangers is classically considered as the problem of "the order of love."

I place importance on love and personal commitment in the family knowing that the social dynamic of poverty and joblessness is a demoralizing force that good families have difficulty overcoming. Discussion of a "new familialism" may ring hollow in the abyss of poverty. While familial failure and irresponsible behaviors can exacerbate economic and social problems, writing on the topic of familial love without strongly asserting the need for social and economic justice does a disservice to parents who have little opportunity to broaden a child's horizons and counter the malaise of boredom and despair.

Philosophers and theologians in our time have had much to say about the sphere of strangers but relatively little about the familial sphere or how these sphere are related, if at all.[1] The prominent theologians of love in this century, such as Anders Nygren and Reinhold Niebuhr, have written about love with little or no attention to familial forms of it such as parental or filial loves.[2] This is remarkable because the familial metaphors of parents and children inform so much of the Hebrew Bible and the New Testament. So we have rather little to go on when it comes to the familial sphere in a time when we seem especially to need it, although there are some signposts in the literature. Gender studies, for instance, have begun to examine motherly and fatherly love.

Anyone writing about familial love and ethics must offer some opening clarification of their basic standpoint. *First,* the revaluing of children requires a new nuclear familialism—not to exclude extended families where they still exist—consistent with gender role equality and the gains of women as well as with the obvious truth that families often need significant social support. Across the nation and the political spectrum there is concern with the parenting deficit that harms children and the community.[3] Family sociologist David Popenoe is one of many who have pointed out the long-term psychological, moral, economic, and behavioral costs for many children who face marital dissolution.[4]

I reject the traditionalist imposition of patriarchal values that often harm married women and have partly fomented the decline of the nuclear family; yet for a variety of important reasons children do best with *both* fathers and mothers and therefore a strong family is important to the future. A vast empirical evidence cited by the nonpartisan National Commission on Children in its 1991 report to the nation indicates that male adolescents who are fatherless lack their essential mentor and role model, and suffer the consequences in higher criminal behavior, serious psychological problems, educational failure, moral debilitation, and involvement with surrogate fathers in the gang context that is now so damaging in our nation.[5] But it is not just boys who suffer, nor children of any one ethnic or class background. The Commission summarizes the data for all children:

> Families formed by marriage—where two caring adults are committed to one another and to their children—provide the best environment for bringing children into the world and supporting their growth and development. Where this commitment is lacking, children are less likely to receive care and nurturing, as well as basic material support. Research on the effects of single parenthood confirms that children who grow up without the support and personal involvement of both parents are more vulnerable to problems throughout childhood and into their adult lives.[6]

The Commission does not say that all children in single-parent families are affected in the same way. It indicates that at most ages problems are more pronounced for sons than for daughters, since most single-parent families are headed by mothers. I must immediately add that while a capable, mature, established, and financially comfortable woman may do quite well raising a son or daughter as a single parent, nevertheless the huge epidemic of unmarried teenage pregnancy is an unmitigated disaster that no society can sustain. I am impressed by the fundamental precept of parental responsibility put forward by one of my teachers, the late moral philosopher Alan Donagan: "It is impermissible for human beings voluntarily to become parents of a child, and yet to refuse to rear it to a stage of development at which it can independently take part in social life."[7]

Obviously it is wrong to think that in some bygone era parents were always present. In fact, as historian Stephanie Coontz describes, for the American colonial family high mortality rates meant that the average length of marriage was less than twelve years and one-third to one-half of children lost a parent before they reached the age of 21. In 1940, moreover, 10 percent of American children did not live with either parent, contrasted with only one in 20 today. So it is difficult to argue that we must go back to some golden age to recover the family. Coontz points out that even in the 1950s, when the American economy allowed for real rises in income, familialism "was often achieved at enormous cost to the wife, who was expected to subordinate her own needs and aspirations to those of both her husband and her children."[8]

The guiding principles of a new familialism that looks forward rather than backward are (a) children first and (b) fairness in gender roles, allowing women the same economic, social, and political opportunities as men if they wish them. Increasingly, both the left and the right in our American political spectrum recognize the social importance of the nuclear family for children and worry about the large numbers of young people who as a result of social conditions and the parenting deficit may never be able to assume constructive places in society.

My emphasis on the importance of the nuclear family, which is in many respects enhanced by embeddedness in the now rare extended family, does not entail that single parents and their children fall outside a broad definition of "the family." However, I accept no definition of family so wide as, for example, "any caring relationship," nor do I think that there are any effective substitutes for the social arrangement of the nuclear family in which fathers and mothers together create a stable life for their children.

Second, what do I mean by "love," an overused word that seems to mean whatever the user wishes? Love is manifested in solicitude (anxious concern) for the welfare of self and others, and usually in a delight in the presence of the other. Love is an abrogation of the self-centered tendency—although not of all concern for the self—and a transfer of interests to the other for his or her own sake on the basis of the other's existence alone, his or her positive properties, or a combination of both. Love is the foundation of all moral idealism, i.e., of acts that surpass the minimal requirement of "do no harm." Adherence to nonmaleficence can be prompted by appeals to prudential long-term or enlightened self-interest, since a society that fails to create powerful restraints on wanton harms or deception is one in which no person could long survive, as the philosopher Thomas Hobbes underscored. But love goes beyond prudential moral minimalism because it represents a shift of the self toward actions for the good of others, and is a much more exacting standard than "do no harm." Love requires the acceptance of a self-sacrifice justly limited by reasonable degrees of self-concern, lest love become oppressive and destructive of the agent.

Clearly love requires the abrogation of selfishness, but it is a mistake to confuse the valid ideal of unselfishness with selflessness, its invalid exaggeration. The unraveling of some families is the result of the mistaken assumption that women, idealized as "ministering angels" in nineteenth-century America, should sacrifice any and all self-concern in order to serve others. Selflessness violates the structures of most social existence, and obscures the extent to which self-concern or care of the self is necessary for love of the other to be sustained in commitment. Moreover, selflessness is questionable because it invites exploitation of the moral agent, and fails to correct the other's harmful behavior. Feminism, psychology, philosophy and theology increasingly converge on this point. It is imperative to analyze intermediate norms between self-preference and radical self-denial, such as parity, other-preference, and self-subordination.[9] There are surely in every age tendencies toward solipsism, i.e., extreme indulgence of and concern with self at the expense of social relationships that demand self-sacrifice. The only value of selflessness might be strategic, as a counterpoint to solipsism.

Many partial descriptions of love can be combined to suggest that, building on a foundation of solicitude, love includes joy, compassion, commitment, and respect: love rejoices in the existence, growth, and presence of the other; love responds supportively to suffering, although present in the absence of suffering; love

5

is loyal and patient to a significant extent; love honors the other's freedom, integrity, and individuality while encouraging the other's good. The solicitude of love can be grounded on voluntary bestowal, on appraisal of attractive qualities, and on the instincts of natural relationships and especially of parental love.

Third, whom do I mean by the stranger? The stranger might be a distant acquaintance or an utterly unknown person encountered by chance. We see strangers every day and demonstrate some concern for them as human beings. There are those who seem truly to love the stranger, devoting a life to caring for the unknown other without any demands for reciprocity. There are saints who seem to manifest an active love for everyone they encounter. William James describes saintly affectivity even for the enemy or those who are personally loathsome.[10] Edith Wyschogrod suggests correctly that the saintly dissolution of self-centeredness is critical for ethics in postmodernity.[11] Yet most of us live our lives and encounter our moral dilemmas in the familial sphere, often unconcerned with the stranger. An insular new familialism does too little good for the stranger and therefore presents the problem of the order of love. Familialism ought never to provide an excuse for apathy to the fate of strangers. Indeed, the family should be a school of love where we learn to cultivate the solicitude that can embrace society and the children who are not our own.

Spheres of Love

What precisely is meant by "spheres" of love? There are two spheres of love. The first, the sphere of personal ethics, is characterized by special relations. Partiality, special obligations, and proximity over extended periods of time roughly define the moral texture of this sphere—we know one another, often deeply. Marriage, parental love, filial love, and friendship lie within the field of personal ethics. The second sphere is that of impersonal ethics, characterized by love for those whom we often do not know in the least. This interweaves with social ethics, the concern with justice and basic social structures. Love of the remote, impartiality, and

6

obligations to strangers lie within the sphere of impersonal ethics. Sometimes a person who was a stranger becomes a friend, moving inward from one sphere to the other, and sometimes people can drift apart.

In a number of religious and philosophical traditions, particular and exclusive forms of love are appropriately haunted by the requirement of radical universal love. But in recent decades, so-called "special relations" and reciprocities have begun to be recognized in philosophical and religious ethics as having moral value. No moral calculus indicates the proper balance between love for those near and dear and love for strangers. However, love for strangers should never be fully eclipsed by special relations.[12]

These two spheres compete for our moral attention, and well they should, for they are both proper areas for love's compass. No philosopher or theologian of whom I am aware has tried to systematically prioritize obligations between these two spheres, and this may be impossible because people are heterogeneous and no inflexible ordering of loves would be applicable. Nicolai Hartmann, for example, offered no moral calculus to balance these spheres, but did offer a principle of general symmetry between "personal love" and "love of the remote."[13] In a related philosophical discussion, Bernard Williams has argued against the impartiality of utilitarianism, for it creates a rift between moral obligations and heartfelt personal commitments. Williams thinks this rift violates the "integrity" of the moral agent.[14]

At the heart of this book, then, lies a debate concerning the order of love (*ordo caritatis*), i.e., the balances between love for those near and dear and those who are remote. With respect to Christian ethics, Stephen J. Pope is making an important contribution in this area.[15] Sally B. Purvis argues that while Augustine could easily accept special relations in his order of love, "the agapic normative tradition . . . exemplified in the extreme by Kierkegaard is very uneasy about special relations."[16] If Purvis is correct, the Augustine-Kierkegaard debate juxtaposes two opposing approaches: in the first, particular and preferential relations "function as a sign of and call toward a love more universal in scope"; in the second, we begin with "universal love—true charity and justify particular loves, if at all, on the basis of Christian love in the fullest sense."[17] I side with Augustine.

I have in my previous writings criticized ethicists who seem rather unconcerned with the field of personal love, who view special relations as obstacles to universal commitments.[18] But I do think love for the stranger is important, and that the moral agent who ignores the stranger is probably not terribly effective in the familial sphere either. The two spheres are related, and no integrated moral agent can live a bifurcated existence, loving those near and dear but dismissing outsiders. My emphasis is shaped only by a conviction that the sphere of special relations and personal love needs greater discussion. I urge, however, a symmetry of interest with love for strangers, and a recognition that each sphere of love requires its own moral language and framework.

A book focused on special-relational loves that does not concentrate on friendship is somewhat unusual. Others, however, have already presented systematic recoveries of friendship in Christian ethics, following a time-honored tradition that reaches back to Augustine and the Gospel of John. They include Paul Wadell,[19] Stanley Hauerwas,[20] Gilbert C. Meilaender,[21] and Catherine Keller.[22] In contrast, the familial element in the sphere of personal love has not been deeply considered. Moreover, the growing national debate over the family and the parenting deficit makes a focus on the familial necessary.

Structure of the Book

Chapters 2 through 5 deal with the familial sphere of love, i.e., married love, sexual love, parental love, and filial love. A sixth chapter focuses on circumstances of familial caregiving that test love and can be so exhausting. The seventh chapter is a constructive affirmation of love for the stranger. In bringing the book to a culmination, the eighth chapter considers the theme of the order of love in depth.

Chapter 2 provides the necessary beginning for an ontology of marriage and family. It is a way forward rather than a recovery of fundamentalist traditions of patriarchy. I am concerned with the absence of powerful cultural meanings that encourage commitment in marriage, although I am fully cognizant of the justice of divorce considered casuistically. Although novel, a revised theism that makes equalitarian marriage reflective of God's own nature seems worthy of discussion. If numerous theologians believe that the return of the feminine aspect of the deity is a necessary condition for a wider cultural transition from patriarchy, then why not apply this to marriage? Throughout this chapter I am consistent with Susan Moller Okin's splendid discussion of justice and equality in marriage and the family.[23] I at no time support the dictum that the role of women is limited to the home. Nor do I imply any bias against those individuals who are called to singleness rather than marriage, for singleness is a time-honored vocation. I urge tolerance of those who are driven by various factors both genetic and psychosocial toward same-sex relations.

But my interest is in the heterosexual marriages that most of us experience and that naturally unfold into biological and social parenthood. I am in full agreement with James M. Gustafson when he calls for renewed attention to marriage and family as communities: "Even the casual reader of literature produced by Christian ethicians, for example, knows that far more attention has been given to homosexuality, abortion, and pre- and extra-marital sexual relationships than to marriage and family as communities and institutions." As Gustafson further writes, "God is enabling and requiring us, as participants in the interdependence of marriage and family, to be stewards, deputies, or custodians of one another and of life itself."[24] Much attention has been given to same-sex relationships in recent writings in Christian ethics, but marriage and family in the heterosexual framework that is the everyday center of most people's moral lives should not be a forgotten topic.

Chapter 3 takes up the theme of sex and love within marriage. While affirming the body, I am also keenly aware of Kant's conclusion that in sexual relations, the "appetite for another human being" can plunge that other into "the depths of misery."[25] I take seriously the obvious truth that harm can and does occur in the domain of sex. My attempt is to reconnect sex and love over against their libertine division. This requires some general cultural criticism.

Chapter 4 is concerned with motherhood and fatherhood. It is partly intended to encourage uncommitted impregnators to become committed fathers, because fatherhood is good for children and also because fatherhood liberates many men from moral immaturity and uncommitment. My sister intended a compliment some years ago when she said that she liked me much more after I became a father; I too felt that fatherhood taught me about responsibility in ways that no other experience in my life had. I will comment on the role of caring fatherhood as redemptive for men insofar as it directs them away from the meaningless pursuits, and creates a uniquely intense solicitude for another, i.e., the child. It is important for ethics to focus greater attention on parenthood, since there is a perennial tendency to violate the covenant of love with our children. It is astounding, for example, how many women students in my classes are forced to work long hours at menial jobs around the university because their fathers refuse to provide child support after divorce. Fatherlessness is a major social problem that is receiving increasing attention. While in 1960 5 percent of children lived apart from their fathers, by 1990 25 percent did. Among other negative results, 70 percent of all juveniles in state reform institutions are from fatherless homes, and the school dropout rate is twice as high for these young people as for others.[26] Ironically, as I shall point out, in the eighteenth century most childrearing was done by fathers.[27]

Chapter 5 deals with the reciprocation of parental love on the part of children. The extent to which filial love can be expected of children is discussed within a framework of intergenerational harmonies. I argue that filial love is entirely contingent on parental love, and that in the absence of the latter the former should not be expected. Filial love is elicited by parents, the *causa efficiens*.

Chapter 6 deals with married, parental, and filial loves in light of the need for and limits on self-denial. When the beloved becomes a significant burden, love is tested. While I think there are reasonable limits to the amount of self-sacrifice that can be expected of any person, I also hold that self-sacrifice is the *sine qua non* of all meaningful love, and that no stable bonds can endure without it. The Pauline injunction to "bear one another's burdens," especially in times of chronic illness, is valid, although surely this injunction can be misused and manipulative, especially of women.

Chapter 7 is written for the reader who has had enough of the sphere of familial love and wants to have something said about love for the stranger. The chapter focuses on neighbor-love regardless of proximity, interweaving the related discussion of conditionality and unconditionality in love. Because I write from a theological framework, and because I believe that the fellowship of believers is essential for the empowering of love for the stranger, I emphasize the interface between the community of faith and those outside it. Moreover, I point out that while unconditional love is perfectly appropriate with respect to the psychophysical needs of the stranger, when it comes to the human-God relation unconditional love must often be expressed as though it were conditional.

Chapter 8 relates the familial sphere of personal ethics to the love for those we do not know. I do not resolve the tension that sometimes exists between them, but I do provide a perspective on why we sometimes have great difficulty loving those who are close to us while waxing eloquent about love for the stranger. This is not to suggest that genuine universal love for humanity is less than an extraordinary and high moral ideal. I am concerned with the inconsistency of failing in proximate relations even while succeeding in remote ones. Few things are more tragic than the successful philanthropist who is a miserable husband and father.

Of course the neighbor is admittedly *every* man and woman, after the injunction "Love your neighbor as yourself" (Lk. 10:27). There is also love for enemies, "Love your enemies and pray for your persecutors" (Mt. 5:44). Religion at its best does break through from the sphere of familial love and friendship to a universal field of impersonal love, yet this does not mean that religious ethics can afford to ignore familial relations and questions of ordered love.

Familial Love as Obstacle?

This book is mostly about familial relations. Ethicists call such relations "special" because they are not impartial or subsumed under some impartial ethical rule, such as "the greatest happiness of the greatest number," that counts the interests of each individual anonymously. In other words, "special" is related to specificity; since these special loves have a *specific* object, they are determinate, not generic. Critics have often devalued them as obstacles to universal impartiality, and as emotion-laden. But I disagree with such critics; I use the word "special" favorably in the sense of unique, highly valuable, and cherished contexts for moral idealism in the form of love, and of caring emotion without which the moral life is impossible. And since so much of moral experience revolves around familial bonds, friendships, or other companionate loves (the word *companion* is derived from the Latin for "with bread," referring to the fellowship between those who share a meal together), these relationships are often at the very center of our everyday lives.

Readers will find in the last two chapters of this book considerable attention to universal love for humanity as such. While I do have a suspicion of assertions of love for humanity, this is only when they hide a failure in loving those who are near and should be dear, as Camus suggested in the person of the friendless Clamance.[28] The parent who has no love for his or her child, yet who waxes eloquent about love for the stranger, does not impress me. I hold that human beings generally learn about love concretely in special relations, and that true love for humanity is often, though not necessarily, an expansion of this learning. Universal love for humanity is a tremendously important moral ideal, but one that for most of us must be built up step by step from what is learned in committed special relations. Thus do the last lines of Alexander Pope's *Essay on Man* read:

> God loves from whole to parts: but human soul
> Must rise from individual to the whole.

Self-love but serves the virtuous mind to wake,
As the small pebble stirs the peaceful lake;
The centre moved, a circle strait succeeds,
Another still, and still another spreads;
Friend, parent, neighbor, first it will embrace;
His country next; and next all human race.

Many readers will find Pope's hopeful movement of love from those near and dear to those far and unknown too naive, for there are many small circles in which the self limits itself in love and forgets the outsider. Yet it still seems that we learn about love in the special ties that both bind and instruct. By Sissela Bok's interpretation, even Kant allows that "friendship of mankind in general" begins in smaller moral friendships.[29]

Finally, it must be acknowledged that Christian ethics has struggled with the familial partly because of the influential "hard sayings" of Jesus in Matthew 10 that seem to condemn this sphere. However, this struggle is misplaced. It is of course true that these words are attributed to Jesus:

> No man is worthy of me who cares more for father or mother than for me; no man is worthy of me who cares for son or daughter; no man is worthy of me who does not take up his cross and walk in my footsteps. By gaining his life for my sake a man will lose it; by losing his life for my sake, he will gain it. (Mt. 10:37–39)

The hard sayings continue: he brings a sword rather than peace to the family, for he will set son against father and daughter against mother, and warns that the follower "will find enemies under his own roof" (Mt. 10:35–36).

But these passages must be placed in context. Jesus demonstrated an exceptional reverence for the family, as evidenced by his statements on marriage (e.g., Mk. 10) and parental love (e.g., Mt. 7:9–11). Often in his preaching the family provides the nearest human analogy to that divine order he sought to reveal. The hard sayings do *not* contradict this; rather, they simply put familial loves on a penultimate level because of the urgency of spreading the news of the kingdom. The hard sayings in Matthew's gospel are recorded as part of Jesus' missionary marching orders to his disciples just before they set out in all directions to preach an original and controversial truth. He was preparing them for persecution and for the antipathies that may, but need not, result when the member of a family converts to a socially unaccepted new religious movement. Relatives are typically slow to accept one another's new religious enthusiasms; the more likely results are acrimony and division. This was as much the case in the early days of the sect of the Nazarene as it is today. The disciples would themselves have to set aside familial loves for the time being, and so also would those they converted.

But this division in no way detracts from the moral centrality of the family with regard to the basic teachings of Jesus. If families do divide, this is justified by the hard sayings, because religious loyalties must outweigh familial ones when the latter regrettably conflict with the former. So the hard sayings do not undercut the theological and ethical importance of the family, although they raise questions about the order of our loyalties and loves that we must honestly deal with.

My interest in the theology and ethics of marriage emerges in part from reflection on E. P. Sanders's widely acclaimed *Jesus and Judaism*. For purposes of this book, suffice it to note that according to Sanders, Jesus' kingdom entailed "a decisive future event which will result in a recognizable social order involving Jesus' disciples and presumably Jesus himself."[30] Jesus saw himself as God's "last messenger before the establishment of the kingdom," and he looked for a "new order" created by an act of God coincident with his own mission:

> In the new order the twelve tribes would be reassembled, there would be a new temple, force of arms would not be needed, divorce would be neither necessary nor permitted, outcasts—even the wicked—would have a place, and Jesus and his disciples—the poor, meek and lowly—would have the leading role.[31]

As a part of this new order, which seems to be a restoration or "renewal of the created order," marriage is especially significant. Sanders argues at length that "the long form of the tradition about divorce, which includes the appeal to Gen. 1.27 and 2.24 (Matt. 19.3–9//Mark 10.2–12), or something very like it, represents Jesus' original saying."[32] Jesus' prohibition against divorce is part of a kingdom world view, and is not to be understood "as an interim ethic nor as an ideal goal which will never be reached, but as a serious decree for a new age and a new order."[33] The Mosaic dispensation was inadequate:

> The prohibition shows that Jesus expected there to be a better order. That this was based on the view that the new would duplicate in some ways the original creation is possible but not certain. Yet the implied expectation of a new and better order is itself eschatological.[34]

The chapters to follow may be interpreted as reflection on why Jesus may have taught that marriage, and, as we shall see, parenthood, are so religiously and morally significant.

Married
Love

In a just society, the structure and practices of families must give women the same opportunities as men to develop their capacities, to participate in political power and influence choices, and to be economically secure. But in addition to this, families must be just because of the vast influence that they have on the moral development of children.

SUSAN MOLLER OKIN, *Justice, Gender, and the Family*

In nature we find God, we do not only infer from nature what God must be like, but when we see nature truly, we see God self-manifested in and through it. Yet the self-revelation so given is incomplete and inadequate. Personality can only reveal itself in persons. Consequently, it is specially in human nature—in men and women—that we see God.

WILLIAM TEMPLE, *Nature, Man and God*

This chapter seeks to construct a framework of meaning that can empower faithful married love. Religiously, it places married love under the sacred canopy of dyadic theism, a motherly-fatherly God, so that marriage represents a form of human completion that reflects the divine; morally, it interprets married love as a crucible in which caring is learned and from which it can be extended. Human sexual behavior is always potentially chaotic and can be expressed in extraordinarily assorted ways. A task of a successful ethics is to construct meanings that order sexual behavior for stable marriage, because otherwise children are harmed and the wider community suffers a lost generation. Summarizing the current data, Amitai Etzioni concludes that while divorces ought not to be condemned, "easy divorces for parents" are in general contrary to the interest of children and community, and even of spouses themselves.[1] (The now empirically established negative impact of the parenting deficit on American children and society is the topic of chapter 4.) Marriage fails for many reasons, one of which is the lack of a foundation in meanings of any ultimate significance.

Without such a foundation, we lack any account of why we would consider committing ourselves to a lifelong relationship under the same roof with someone who is ultimately a relational challenge and may at times seriously burden us from the vantage point of the individualistic ideology of self-actualization. The vow "until death do us part" is clearly irrational if all we want is self-actualization and happiness. Without a sacred canopy, the natural history of marriage will often result in eventual dissolution, and why not? A faithful and lasting marriage is a dutiful act, especially as the human lifespan increases.

The ideal of marriage includes the public and purposeful union with a member of the opposite sex intended as a life partnership. Ours is a time for valid reassessment of gender roles and justice within marriage and family, but to question the essential viability of marriage goes too far. Though subject to some cross-cultural variations, marriage serves as a uniquely valued context for responsible intimacy and as a necessary stable context for parenting. Parental love is at the very center of any adequate ethics because the memories of caring, comfort, and sustenance are carried by the child throughout life, and without these memories there is little hope for the moral life. Sex is the basis for species survival; parental love is the basis upon which moral civilization rests. Most issues facing marriage have to do with modification of gender roles in the context of modern society and its demands, and with the removal of behaviors oppressive to women. But a good marriage itself remains an almost unanimous ideal, and this indicates something important about human beings.

Yet without a sacred canopy, marriage has been difficult to sustain. Today half of marriages in the United States end in divorce; the answer to this problem is not the retrieval of traditions of marriage that have been unfair to women, as is the intent in various forms of fundamentalism. Rather, the full dignity of marriage must be newly articulated in ways that it has not been in the past, although aspects of various traditions can be retained.

I will not detail the historically important theological ethical arguments on behalf of married love and fidelity, since these are already stated in the literature.[2] The notion that marriage is worthy of religious solemnization remains of lasting importance. Following the Book of Common Prayer liturgy on "Solemnization of Matrimony" as an example of Christian thought, Edward S. Gleason asserts that marriage "has to do with God," "is part of the original and natural order of things," is an essentially mysterious union like the mystical one between Christ and the church, should be entered reverently with the exchange of vows, and is a place where God dwells.[3] The act of entering marriage with solemnity is morally significant, since this involves a commitment to the very idea of marriage as a permanent tie. Solemnization marks marriage as an area of ultimate theological concern and a rite of passage rather than of casualness. I find nothing to disagree with in Gleason's useful summary. Etzioni emphasizes the importance of churches and synagogues in counseling young people about marriage and introducing "waiting periods" so that they can be better prepared for it.[4]

If Gleason is correct, and I think he is, then Christianity is countercultural, for the solemnization of marriage is a stark contrast to the wider culture's trivialization of marriage as fleeting. Philip Turner states that Christianity provides marriage with the theological roots that are "an alternative to a society which seems increasingly incapable of anything more than 'limited engagements.'"

He stresses that love seeks constancy and security, and that "only something like a vow can give it the surety it requires."[5] The vows of marriage provide assurance that sexual desire will not be allowed to focus its glance on others, and they "locate us within a public world that is bigger and more powerful than our own private space" and make us publicly accountable. Turner refers to a process of maturing in love that takes time, commitment, and fidelity. This is particularly important, for without loyalty to the other through hard times we need never learn compassion or respect under difficult conditions.

In no way do I wish to diminish the significance of these classical theological arguments on behalf of marriage. I do want to add to them in the light of dyadic theism, since so much contemporary religious thought has moved to including the feminine in God. Moreover, I want to relate marriage to loves for those outside it, for I suspect that inattention to the ethics of married love is partly related to a concern that such love is an obstacle rather than a means toward love for the stranger.

Dyadic Theism: Religious Meaning

The image of a mother-father God can bestow additional religious meaning on marriage. This is because under such an image, wife and husband conjoined reflect the feminine and masculine aspects of God. The notion of marriage as *in imagine Dei* suggests a heuristic key into the rigor with which Jesus of Nazareth condemned divorce as a violation of a profound unity. While Moses permitted divorce "by note of dismissal," Jesus claims this was only because "your minds were closed; but in the beginning, at the creation, God made them male and female" (Mk. 10:5–7). This indicates that permanence is the ideal from the beginning of creation and is part of the original purpose of God: "What God has joined together man must not separate" (Mk. 10:9). The appeal here is to creation and to a dyadic ontology; marriage in original equality and freedom is an indissoluble unity (Mk. 10:12). Geoffrey Parrinder draws on Mark 10 to conclude that Jesus affirmed monogamy as originally ordained by God. Jesus "seems to have been looking to the purpose of creation, and he took the divine pattern of the creation of man and woman in singleness and unity."[6] Of course Judaism does not think of God as a sexual being, as two entities wrapped in embrace. But human sexuality and the union of man and woman in purposeful freedom is meaningfully linked with divine likeness and the pattern of God in creation.

The Christian moral tradition has never gone so far as to consider the idea of human perfection partly in terms of the ordinance of marriage. R. Newton Flew's classical study of the idea of perfection in Christian theology covers a range of thought from the early church to modernity, and in all cases images of perfection concern the individual.[7] I intimate an ideal of dyadic human perfection in and through marriage, drawing on the emerging image of a feminine-masculine, mother-father God in contemporary theology.[8]

At stake in married love may be one aspect of the image of God itself. This would explain why Jesus took the permanence of marriage so much more seriously than many find it comfortable to acknowledge. The image of God in human beings may be to some extent manifest in the dyadic communion of faithful married love, and the spiritual meaning of marriage can be understood in these terms. Classically, Christianity has discerned the image of God in human rational nature, in the ability to love, or in some other inherent characteristic of human beings that pertains to individuals as such. But add to the classical image of God in the particular *individual* the notion that "God created man in his image, male and female created he them" (Gn. 1:27). This passage from the creation account—a fit alternative to the passages indicating that Eve was created from the rib of Adam and is by implication subservient to him—suggests that woman and man together constitute the image of God. An expression of the image of God would then be the conjugal dyad of wife and husband.

A weakness in traditional Christian thought about marriage has been not in accepting the influential and highly Jewish appeal of Jesus to the order of creation, but in linking this order to influential passages in the Pauline Ephesians 5:21–33—passages exegetes do not consider Paul's own. Here wives must be "subject to your husbands" for "man is the head of woman." Combined with appeal to the order of creation, this Pauline distortion unfortunately justified patriarchy. Thus when Martin Luther based his ethics of marriage on Genesis 1:27, "So God created man . . . male and female he created them," and then appealed to the "divine ordinance" of procreation, he insisted that a woman be fully obedient to her husband in all things.[9]

The exegetical studies of Galatians 3:26–28, such as those of Elisabeth S. Fiorenza and Hans Dieter Betz, highlight the social and political implications of Christian freedom, and these implications have clear relevance to marriage.[10] The passage "Wives be subject to your husbands as is fitting in the Lord" (Col. 3:18) and other such Pauline passages are neither directly attributable to Paul nor acceptable ethically. There would be fewer objections to the notion of marriage as an ordinance of creation if it were coupled with Galatians 3:26–28 rather than with Ephesians.

Is conjugal love the mark of God in creation? Emil Brunner, while unacceptably patriarchal, hints at a meaning of marriage in dyadic theism, although he did not develop this. He writes of basing marriage "on something higher; that is, on the Divine order of creation." Jesus Himself, "when He speaks authoritatively about marriage, appeals to this order." Brunner describes a "trinity of being we call the human structure of existence," i.e., Father, Mother, and Child.[11] There is much of value in the Genesis notion of the ordinance of creation imposed "from the beginning" (Mt. 19:4–5) upon the otherwise chaotic disorderings that human beings are capable of. For Brunner marriage is more than a contractual agreement or a mutual attraction; it carries connotations about the very character of divine purpose in creation and about a complementary union that enables human beings to participate in creation.

Among the better examples of analogical thinking that leads to dyadic theism is that of the Shaker theologian James Prescott. A convert to Shakerism in 1826, Prescott articulated a dyadic theism as follows:

The Shakers hold that God is dual, male and female, mother and father; they hold that these two attributes exist in the deity; that these two attributes are exhibited throughout the universe of God; that wherever we turn our eyes, we behold two principles, male and female.[12]

Prescott argued that "the duality of God is established in holy writ," drawing on Genesis 1:27 and Romans 1:20. He prayed like all Shakers, "Our Father and Mother which art in Heaven." The Shakers did not marry because sex was considered sinful, but the analogical structures of their thinking are nevertheless instructive.

There is no natural theology that could logically persuade any rationalist that something of God's character is evident in creation. *All natural theology is fideistic,* a matter of intuition, an example of the human analogical imagination envisioning the character of the deity through comparisons with human experiences and perceptions.[13] However philosophically questionable, religious people in various traditions have anyway intuited that nature is a signpost to God. From the Platonic perspective, the natural world results from divine craftsmanship, and nature is a means of discovering divine goodness (*Laws* Bk. X. 889a–890b). Isaac Newton understood mathematical principles as products of divine ordinance. The union of theology and natural science known as natural theology was prominent in the eighteenth century, most notably in the theology of William Paley: nature is divine artifice, revealing the character of the creator. Natural theology fell to the skepticism of the French *philosophes,* and Darwin put an end to the idea of God as "first cause." Hume was especially critical of inference from creation to creator, and in the light of his critique all natural theology must be construed as intimation rather than logic.

Again, there is no logical argument by which to infer theism from these natural observations; moreover, there will be many who are already theists but reject the correlation between a pattern of creation and the nature of the creator. But for those who intuit something of God's nature in the pattern of the creation, the *a posteriori* movement from effect back to the cause is attractive.

Exceptions to the ordinance of marriage are permissible (Mt. 19:10–12), a theme that is echoed in Paul's interim ethic counseling celibacy (1 Cor. 7:25–35), for he thought the world soon to end and considered marriage a hindrance to evangelical activity, fitting only for those who absolutely could not live without it. God calls some people to singleness. But marriage remains the essential ordinance. Cecil John Cadoux places celibacy in a perspective that retains marriage as the ideal:

> Jesus does not, however, exalt celibacy as an ideal state for man generally or even for his own disciples. To do so would have been to contradict his own words as to the Divine origin and sanction of marriage. But he does realize that, under the conditions then existing, not only the marriage-tie, but any family bond, might quite easily become a hindrance to loyal discipleship and zealous service of the Kingdom; and he insists with great emphasis on the relative subordination of such domestic claims.[14]

Cadoux adds that a temporary emphasis on celibacy is "not altogether unnatural in a time of religious enthusiasm."[15] While Paul in general favored celibacy, Cadoux attributes this entirely to Paul's beliefs about the imminent termination of the present world. The more basic teaching of Jesus is the prohibition of divorce.

Dyadic Theism: Feminist Concerns

Some feminists rightly reject dyadic theism as unfitting since it can be deeply hierarchical and has often been so in the past, for example in the Asian mode of Yang (male, dominance) and Yin (female, passivity). However, a deeply equalitarian dyadic theism that encourages the demise of all hierarchy in marriage remains possible. The dyadic structure of creation is indicated by paired complements. There is something about the universe that is akin to music, with tones that are treble or bass, with aspects of concavity or protrusion. Barbara E. Reed suggests an equalitarian reinterpretation of Taoism: "There are two sides, but they depend on each other for existence. The goal is the balancing of the two sides, the mutual interaction of the two forces." In such complementary dualism, "neither side is better than nor independent of the other."[16]

Numerous feminist theologians have rightly argued that the church needs to retrieve feminine imagery of God in order for women to exist with self-esteem and equal standing with men in all respects. The National Council of Churches recommended an inclusive language lectionary. Virginia Ramey Mollenkott argued two decades ago that when the Bible is interpreted contextually, the theme of male-female equality pervades, and that this interpretation is essential for equality and mutuality in the church.[17] My intention is to suggest a reflective equilibrium between the symbolically and socially important image of dyadic theism and marriage, where it can serve as a framework for freedom, equality, and commitment just as powerfully as it can in the church.

Language about God is generally analogical, drawing on similarities between what is known and what is unknown, as will be examined more closely in chapter 5. In both Judaism and Christianity, God-talk frequently draws on analogy to marriage and family, probably because this is such a central human experience. Elaine H. Pagels points out that in the Gnostic Gospels, God is sometimes envisioned as "both divine Father and Mother," and the Trinity interpreted as "Father, Mother, Son."[18] Phyllis Trible points out that in the Hebrew Bible maternal images are frequently applied to God in addition to paternal ones.[19] Her critique allows the maternal metaphor to emerge, as does the discussion of historical women who envisioned a female and maternal God. Included in this discussion are Saint Bridget of Sweden (c. 1302–1373) and Julian of Norwich (d. after 1415).

An image of God as both motherly and fatherly, female and male, will not be useful in solving the problem of gender inequities unless hierarchy is removed. But as Mollenkott writes, "Inclusive God-language is a step in the right direction of that enrichment. It is only a beginning, but on the other hand it *is* a beginning." She suggests that the Lord's prayer might be addressed to "Our Father/Mother [or Mother/Father] who is in Heaven."[20]

Critics of dyadic theism will rightly claim that it in no way ensures an end to patriarchy—at least dyadic theism as we have known it historically in American religion—and may even further ensconce it in consciousness. For example, in her study of Shaker theology and community, Linda A. Mercadante points out that the Shaker image of female/male God did not result in women serving as elders. While the Shakers rejected the classical trinitarian understanding of God because "they believed it was essentially masculinist," their polity remained masculinist to a large extent, despite a female messiah figure.[21] A hierarchical dyadic theism would serve only to further patriarchy.

Nevertheless, there is potential practical merit for dyadic theism in relation to marriage consistent with equality in gender roles. This discussion of dyadic theism must never mask a way back to traditional patriarchy, but it must be an authentic way forward that retains all the advances hard won by feminism.

A Degree of Permanence

Marriage fails for many reasons, one of which is a weak foundation. The permanence that is necessary if love is to be learned is interrupted by lack of religious and moral purpose. But in modern culture, the notion of wedlock was unlocked for good reasons, especially given the physical and psychological oppression of women. The pendulum had to swing, and swing it did. Moral progress in the area of justice in marriage has been very slow, and utterly rejected by many traditions. The sacred canopy that I am attempting to construct above marriage would prove destructive if coupled with patriarchal oppression. While some forms of feminism have been decried as solipsistic and antagonistic to marriage, the fact is that historical patriarchy is one root of current trends toward marital dissolution. So any discussion of permanence must be qualified, however much it is necessary for the future of children.

The ideal of permanence is articulated in the phrase "The two shall become one flesh" (Gn. 2:24). Yet permanence can go too far. For the idea of permanence without exceptions has meant historically that women have no recourse to divorce. One of the most widely used and influential American textbooks in ethics was written in 1835 by Francis Wayland, president of Brown University. His assertion about divorce, extrapolated from Matthew 19:3–9, is: "The contract is for life, and is dissoluble for one cause only, the cause of whoredom."[22] Absolutist and utterly inattentive to "hard cases," we today rightfully attend to the casuistry of domestic violence, incest, sexual abuse, and psychological repression of women. Absolutism's most forceful spokesperson in modern times is Denis de Rougemont, who asserts that a religious vow is taken for "time and eternity," which means it makes no allowances for casuistical exceptions, nor is the goal of marriage the superficial "happiness" contingent on the ups and downs of relationship.[23] This position is extreme.

Nevertheless, without going back to absolutism or succumbing to the urge to uncritically reappropriate past tradition, our current culture needs to affirm some shared values regarding the general ideal of permanence if lastingness in marriage is to be the rule rather than the exception. De Rougemont was too uncompromising, but he accurately predicted the weakening of marital fidelity, the trivialization of the marriage bond, the overvaluation of passionate love at the expense of lasting companionate love or marital friendship,[24] and the cultural atrophy of marriage as a moral task requiring purposeful decision from the outset.

A crucial *contribution* to permanence is gender justice in marriage, although strict traditionalists wrongly view it as destructive. Traditional Christian teachings on marriage can be corrected by ideas about gender, justice, and the family articulated by Susan Moller Okin.[25] Women are vulnerable in gendered marriage because their social, political, and economic rights to equal opportunity are often violated. It is important that men engage in direct caregiving and nurturing of children, and that women who choose professions and other public roles be able to do so. Okin emphasizes that the unfortunate tolerance of injustice in the wider society is learned and nurtured in unjust family structures. Consistent with

Okin's thrust, Lisa Sowle Cahill dismisses all theological–ethical attempts to narrowly define the roles of men and women in marriage according to theories of biological determinism, arguing in part from empirical studies that "freedom makes impossible and narrow confinement of the expression of the masculine and the feminine to propagative and species–survival functions."[26] In freedom, not every woman will want to pursue a profession, but institutions should make it possible for a woman to pursue both professional and familial roles simultaneously if desired.

Even a marriage constructed on the principles of freedom, equality, justice, and love can gradually become meaningless. Margaret A. Farley, who endorses the "way of fidelity," includes profound loss of meaning as grounds for release from matrimonial promise.[27] But I would ask Farley to elaborate more fully on what the meaning of marriage might be. Is it not a task of theology to construct a sacred meaning for marriage and encourage its permanence while cognizant of some justified divorce? In constructing a theological meaning for marriage, I by no means want to underestimate the problems of domestic violence and repression, nor do I want to support traditional church counsel for women that these harms are their "cross to bear" and that the appropriate response is self-sacrifice. I do not define love primarily in terms of self-sacrifice, but rather as solicitude. Yet obviously no marriage can succeed without patience and sacrifice within limits that will vary according to the individual.

Feminists have rightly rejected definitions of love in terms of self-sacrifice at the expense of reasonable self-concern. While there is a need to encourage commitment in marriage, there will always be the "hard cases" in which divorce is justified. But my interest is in a possible theological meaning that can provide marriage with a *raison d'être* in a time when the dissolution of marriages for trivial and selfish reasons is commonplace, often at the emotional expense of children. A task of any marriage has been, is, and always will be moral growth in the work of sustaining commitment and solicitude even when this is not easy. The dissolution of marriage for trivial reasons makes a mockery of the moral progress open to married people and fails to put the interests of children first. Father-lessness or motherlessness is not a thing that children desire.

The Limits of Meaning in Romanticism

Conjugal love *in imagine Dei* is rooted in a religious world view. Such love is not necessarily inimical to romanticism, to "falling in love." However, romantic infatuation often wanes, as Stendahl and other consistent romantics frankly acknowledged. Marriage, if in the image of God, is too important to be left on the frail scaffold of romantic love. It must be grounded in deeper meaning and authority.

Christian thought places married love in the tradition of be-stowal.[28] The choice of a partner is usually reason-dependent, i.e., X can provide property-based reasons for loving Y, and vice versa. The attractive properties of the beloved account for the presence of mutual desire. Christianity, however, is skeptical of a strictly property-based and essentially acquisitive relationship, since this leaves love insecure. Either the properties for which X loves Y will disappear, or X may no longer find these properties enticing. So solemnization lifts marriage into the domain of bestowal, of a so-licitousness that is not conditioned by properties in the other. It places marriage in the wider tradition of nonappraising love, and requires the expression of love through compassion, attentive lis-tening, presence, and loyalty. Property-based attractions may en-dure as superstructure, but in most marriages the intensity of these attractions will wane at times, or X will begin to see that there are myriad other more attractive individuals. Thus Stanley Hauerwas is correct to argue that the best marriages may often be the ones in which spouses understand from the outset that you always marry the wrong person: "We never know whom we marry; we just think we do. Or even if we first marry the right person, just give it a while and he or she will change."[29] Hauerwas believes that mar-riage is saved by "contributing to a people through having chil-dren," another topic left for chapter 4.

Romantic love will wax and wane, lacking permanence. Romanticism is, by some interpretations, simply an extension of sexual *eros*. It is an assessment of beauty. All the significant romantic thinkers followed Stendahl in acknowledging that the "crystallizations of passion-love," which for a time adorn the beloved with various perfections, inevitably melt away, at which point movement to another object of adornment is inevitable.[30] It has been said that for marriage to persist, desire and appraisal must give way to benevolence and bestowal. In Christian language, spouses become Christ to one another.

Conjugal love *in imagine Dei* is distinguishable from romantic obsession, for it has a spiritual and rational basis. Our culture requires a shift away from the modern socially inculcated assumption that "being in love" is all that gives marriage meaning. Deeper meanings are needed. Can a religious *Weltanschauung* strengthen the marriage bond in our society, where half of marriages result in divorce?

Marriage benefits from the mature spirit of companionate love on a religious journey. Historian Georges Duby cites a synod recommendation from Rouen (1012) that "the husband and wife, fasting, should be blessed in church by the priest, fasting."[31] Marriage under the authority of sacred vows places it on a very different basis from the highly individualistic vicissitudes of romantic love. Married love is in many respects continuous with the sort of friendship love characteristic of a community of believers. It is a companionate love, the joining together as community for a common meal. Even surrounded with meanings, marriage to succeed requires embeddedness in a community with expectations and requirements of marriage.

The heightened romantic-sexual expectations that have popularly come to define conjugal love can lead to divorce, since a departure from them means failure. The respiritualization of marriage is surely countercultural, but nevertheless marriage must be viewed in Christian thought as an opportunity for spiritual growth in the context of a community of shared belief.

Certainly romantic infatuation has meant a moral blindness with respect to humanity as such. The preoccupation with romanticism, so persuasively criticized by Wollstonecraft and Greer, can be destructive of a more universal love for humans as such. Lives have been morally wasted in the "game" of love. An adequate ethic of marriage must connect married love with wider moral commitments.

Conjugal Love and Universal Love

James M. Gustafson writes, "The divine empowering and ordering of life takes place in and through 'nature': through human biological relationships first of all." Human beings participate in "the divine ordering of the world." Contrasting his thought with theological ethicists who make Christian love "virtually synonymous with Kant's principle of respect for persons," Gustafson takes "special" relations more seriously, since "the 'natural' ordering of life has theological and moral dignity."[32] I agree with Gustafson, and have added a revised theism to further enhance the significance of the ordinance of creation.

The married love *in imagine Dei* that I defend leads toward more powerful universal love. It is sustained by a wider community informed by the story of the Good Samaritan. The narrative context of scripture informs the conscience of wife and husband so that they live not just for themselves, but for others in their community and for strangers who are outside it. Married love can be a place for the development of wider loves.

Marriage is then a school of love, as Roger Mehl suggests.[33] There is seldom a concrete universal love without the learning process that successful special relations such as marriage, parenthood, and friendship require. People justify themselves through appeals to abstract universal love, while failing to show genuine (concrete) love for even one person near to them. In chapter 1 I cited Alexander Pope's *Essay on Man*: "God loves from whole to parts; but human soul must rise from individual to the whole." While we are enjoined to serve all of humanity, this cannot be done directly; it can be achieved indirectly through love in special relations of proximity so long as narrow loyalties are held in check by wider ones, including love for humanity and even for nature.

Married love itself is the fruit of experience with other special relations. The arts of sibling love and of friendship love learned before marriage are foundations for successful conjugal love. Married love is thus a concentric circle that flows outward from parental love, the love of children for parents, sibling love, and other special relations. There is a sense in which a marital relationship requires one to love a spouse sometimes as parent, sometimes as child, as brother or sister, or as friend. Married love draws on all these learning experiences. Success in true conjugal love is an educational foundation for the love of humanity.

An excellent articulation of the expansion of conjugal love is provided by the American Baptist theologian Walter Rauschenbusch in a little-known work entitled *Dare We Be Christians?* Rauschenbusch argues that love expands concentrically from a variety of special relations, one of which is conjugal love, "always weaving new combinations of lives" as whole groups or families are connected in "friendly cooperation." Moreover, "the love of fatherhood and motherhood is a divine revelation and a miracle. It is a creative act of God within us." Without this love "children would die like the flies of late summer and the race would perish." From forms of love that have "the support of physical nearness and of constant intercourse and habit" people begin to take an interest in the "chance-met stranger." In sum, "So the love for one man promptly widens out into the love of many and weaves more closely the web of social life."[34] These are remarkable passages because they capture a side of Rauschenbusch that is decidedly not Kantian. Kant's moral agent is ahistorical, stripped of the special relations that develop over time between those in proximity, and abstracted from the familial ties that in reality are such a large part of everyday moral experience. Rauschenbusch was deeply informed by Kant in many respects, but in this text he rejects the Kantian endeavor to transcend empirical anthropology and the human embeddedness in special relations.

Conjugal love, viewed in this light, leads naturally to that form of love that Rauschenbusch considers a "divine revelation" and a "creative act of God in us," motherhood and fatherhood. Of parental love he writes, "Last year it was not; this year it is, and all things are changed. The dry rock of our selfishness has been struck down and the water of sacrificial love pours forth."[35] It is the springing of this powerful form of love that occupies the attention of chapter 4. Daniel Day Williams wrote: "Provision for a stable family structure usually has in view the protection of children. Here again one obvious justification of the monogamous family is that it offers the healthiest community for the growth of children."[36]

The
Misuse
of
Sexual Love

Let's be indulgent and use the word "infirmity," a sort of congenital inability to see in love anything but the physical. That infirmity, after all, was convenient.
    CAMUS, *The Fall*

Love, love, love—all the wretched cant of it, masking egotism, lust, masochism, fantasy under a mythology of sentimental postures, a welter of self-induced miseries and joys, blinding and masking the essential personalities in the frozen gestures of courtship, in the kissing and the dating and the desire, the compliments and the quarrels which vivify its barrenness.
    GERMAINE GREER, *The Female Eunuch*

While we should avoid all prejudice against the human body, the modern cultural assumption that happiness is achieved as a matter of course through sexual liberation from the order of loyal marriage has proved unfounded. Although Christianity has too often viewed sex negatively, its excesses are nevertheless a useful counterpoint to the extreme preeminence of sex in modern secular culture. It has been observed that modern secular culture "envisages man the external phenomenon, his sensual well-being. And increasingly it envisages this well-being in isolation from the objective hierarchy of real and spiritual goods."[1]

Since my aims are constructive rather than expository, I do not intend a full-scale interpretation of the thinkers referred to in this chapter, including Kierkegaard. My argument moves from an emerging hermeneutics of cultural suspicion regarding the casualization of sex and the debilitation of marriage to a second look at the sexual interpretation of the symbolic Fall narrative of Genesis, although one that is entirely free from the misogynist notion that men are less sinful than women. The ethics of sex put forward here is the natural extension of the previous chapter on the meaning of marriage, and will lead to the chapter that follows on parental love.

The Hermeneutics of Cultural Suspicion

Because clinical psychiatrists work close to the pulse of modern culture, their perspectives on the chaos of our time are grounded in medical concern rather than abstraction. Psychiatrist Willard Gaylin describes the current American scenario bluntly:

> While the final score is not yet in, the results so far of this so-called "sexual revolution" are less than reassuring. The Freudian view of human behavior laid the positive groundwork for the liberation of the sexual aspirations of women from both an oppressive personal sense of guilt and the shame and humiliation of social stigmatization. But the only empirical results of that illegitimate offspring of Freudian philosophy, the sexual revolution, seem to be the spread of two sexually transmitted diseases, genital herpes and AIDS; an extraordinary rise in the incidence of cancer of the cervix; and a disastrous epidemic of teenage pregnancies.[2]

Gaylin, a romantic personalist with respect to philosophies of love, opposes "the trend towards highlighting the erotic aspects of sexual intimacy and permitting the separation of sex from intimate social bonds."[3] His personalist philosophy of sex stresses mutual love and a significant fidelity. Not incidentally, in the above passage Gaylin refers to the sexual revolution as the illegitimate offspring of Freudian thought because Freud himself believed in reasonable sexual restraint.

Another prominent psychiatrist, Paul R. Fleischman, writes that if sexual repression dominated the psychological landscape in Freud's Vienna, the current problem is quite the reverse. (On a point of minor correction, one might add that sexual repression dominated the landscape for the *haute bourgeoisie* of Vienna but not for the aristocracy or the peasants and working class.) Fleischman's assessment of current clinical psychiatric practice is central to my concerns:

> Among the hurt and pained in need of help, who may suffer from broken marriages, fluctuating or fallen self-esteem, obsessive constrictions, panicky attachments to parents, bewildering isolation, uncontrolled rages, and haunting depressions, the common denominator is an inability to transcend themselves with care and delight, to reach over and touch another heart.[4]

Fleischman's patients report that they suffer emotionally because they have assumed that genuine love requires sexual intimacy. They then pursue such relations, even when inappropriate, and suffer the consequences. Their experience may be summed up thus:

> The binding together, the touch of person to person, is sought concretely, rather than spiritually, and dyadically rather than communally. The substitution of sexuality for religious life constitutes one of the most prominent and pervasive elements of cultural pathology that a psychotherapist encounters.[5]

Many people seek to touch physically for the sake of sexual intimacy alone, failing to see physical touch as at all expressive of a deeper spiritual meaning. They make sexual intimacy rather than spiritual values the center of their lives.

Such concerns are prominent in current psychiatric circles. They go back at least to Rollo May's criticism of the depersonalizing tendencies of a culture obsessed with sex as a mechanical function and as the mandatory expression of any relationship worth mentioning. May considered the sexual libertarianism of the late 1960s to be a "new straitjacket." He argues that in so-called "free love" we do not learn to love, for such learning is work and requires long-term commitment so that relationships can serve as crucibles of moral development.[6]

Certainly the concerns of many psychiatrists could be applied to earlier periods in this century. Historians John D'Emilio and Estelle B. Freedman have shown that by the mid-1910s assumptions were commonplace in America that the sexual instinct demands constant expression, that restraint is harmful, and that gratification is a more worthy ideal than self-control. Thus, "the shift from a philosophy of continence to one that encouraged indulgence was but one aspect of a larger reorientation that was investing sexuality with a profoundly new importance."[7] Sin was redefined as *not* expressing libido, and all restraint was construed as negating and repressive. Again, this ideology of sex built on Freud, who had considerable disdain for it. The possibility of arguing for sexual restraint without diminishing the glory of sexual *eros* was not contemplated.

And it was in the 1950s that C. S. Lewis, however distanced he may have been from sexual intimacy throughout most of his life, rightly warned against the loss of any serious moral caution regarding sexual intimacy: "Poster after poster, film after film, novel after novel, associate the idea of sexual indulgence with the ideas of health, normality, youth, frankness, and good humour. Now this association is a lie." It is a lie, wrote Lewis, because sexual indulgence without commitment and steadfast love has always been associated with disease, deception, jealousies, and emotional pain. Lewis claimed that our society has lost sight of definitions of love that do not place sexual intimacy at their center, that it has illusory expectations of this intimacy, and that the result is oppressive. He rejected the practice of sexual union when it is isolated "from all the other kinds of union which were intended to go along with it and make up the total union." He complained against the "contemporary propaganda for lust" that makes it appear perverse to resist sexual union out of respect for a lasting and total union.[8] Lewis considered it urgent to articulate nonsexual manifestations of love, such as friendships, parental love (he borrowed the Greek word *storge*), and charity.

Historical nuances aside, popular culture has wrongly abstracted the sexual area from the wider aspects of human personality, and made a mockery of the notion that there are positive physical and emotional advantages in adopting a philosophy of life that places the sexual experience within a committed and trusting relationship. There is, however, a significant movement to rediscover the ethical aspects of sex. In 1980 Gabrielle Brown's immensely successful *The New Celibacy* was first published. In a later edition, Brown points out that the new celibacy is not simply due to fear of AIDS and other sexually transmitted diseases, but to support for the "decasualization of sex." She is concerned with "an overenriched conception of sexual behavior," whereby "people end up thinking they are more sexual than they really are. And they feel they should live up to a false picture of sexuality that has been created as a standard."[9] Even for married couples, Brown suggests that periods of celibacy can serve to reestablish presexual forms of tender communication and love.

Additionally, feminists such as Catherine A. MacKinnon have played an important role in pointing out that proclaimed freedoms in the sexual domain have masked wanton violence, date rape, and other oppression of women.[10] So it is now credible to express suspicions of our sexual culture; this chapter may be understood as a part of an emerging hermeneutics of cultural suspicion that involves people from across the political and ideological spectrum.

Surely the hermeneutics of cultural suspicion can go too far. In the previous chapter marriage was presented as a means of completion and sanctification, so clearly in this context sex must be holy and good. Sex is a gift when integrated into marriage as a means to the fulfillment of redemptive and creative purposes. The early Church Fathers were unable to understand sex as an aspect of religious experience and meaning within marriage, a context in which sex is an essential part of the communion of love between wife, husband, and God. Christianity, in its negative understanding of sex, was not inconsistent with some of Greek and Roman philosophy.[11] It is necessary and praiseworthy that a chorus of Christian ethicists have made progress in asserting the inherent goodness in sexual intimacy. James B. Nelson has been particularly important in debunking traditional Christian tendencies to interpret the body and sex in largely negative terms as obstacles rather than paths to spiritual growth, although I will later argue that Nelson's endorsement of "open marriage" is utterly inconsistent with the best of Christian ethics.[12]

But however much we can agree that sex can contribute to the spiritual life in marriage, this is no warrant to dismiss the hermeneutics of cultural suspicion. If we are to judge from the history of rape, child molestation, infidelity leading to the destruction of families, and countless other moral transgressions that leave victims profoundly harmed, an ideology of the "joys of sex" has tended to obscure significant aspects of reality. I use "ideology" here in the negative sense: facts are systematically ignored and removed from consideration. In our wider secular culture most people "will acknowledge no hierarchy of values" and "will live for the moment in a chaos of pure sensation."[13] Granted that sexual restraint and the culture of control can be unduly morbid and dualistic, it is not mere frivolity that the likes of St. Paul and Augustine, even if excessively dualistic, as well as Buddha and Socrates, all asserted that sexual desires can intoxicate the whole personality to the exclusion of spiritual values and interests. Around sexual desire the churches have built up the vows of marriage, to dominate it lest they be dominated by it.

Human Disorder: Harms Both Spiritual and Moral

Traditions of sexual discipline and control indicate a widespread understanding that sexual desire can impede spiritual and sacred values, reflecting human disorder rather than design. The Pauline notion of a conflict between the law of one's members and the pursuit of the holy is attested by common experience, indicating that the use of sex as a good is not easy for people. Bodily desires can easily muscle aside spiritual and sacred ones. Hence ascetic traditions have emerged so widely in world religious culture. But the aim of restraint, as Kierkegaard argued, is the affirmation of good rather than the prohibition of evil. The task is to bring sexuality "under the qualification of the spirit (here lie all the moral problems of the erotic)."[14] Therefore, I do not see asceticism as an end in itself for most people, but as an interim response to human disorder.

In addition to the tension between unrestraint and the realization of higher values, sexual desire can reduce its objects to mere means. This is the strictly ethical aspect of harm. Kant commented at length on how harmful the "appetite for another human being" can be, and added that "there is no way in which a human being can be made an object of indulgence for another except through sexual impulse." It is a simple fact, Kant contends, that through sexual appetite one human being often plunges another into "the depths of misery," casting him or her aside "as one casts away a lemon which has been sucked dry."[15] The analogy is powerful and fitting. Many look back on their lives with uneasy conscience for nonchalant lies about being committed, for attractions that ruined families, for thinking that the ethics of sex is merely a matter of consent. It is this Kantian sensitivity to the ways in which sexual impulse can reduce women and men to mere means that I take to be the proper message of the symbolic Fall narrative, to be considered in the following section.

Many thinkers, including Plutarch, virtually all the Stoics, and the Physicians also articulated a growing skepticism of unrestrained sexual activity and its consequences for the individual and for society. These views were against the grain of common practice in the Roman Empire of that day. Pride, the desire to dominate others, self-assertion, and egocentrism—all in place of love—can animate sexual desire. Our culture of flight from restraint disguises these realities. Religious ethics should not become trapped by this flight. In the case of sexual ethics and modern culture, the religion of culture may be worse than no religion at all. In recent Christian ethics, the debate over sexual ethics has become especially pointed because so much is at stake.

The Fall

The French theologian Jean Danielou offered this assessment of Catholic thought: "A majority of critics underline the fact that sin has a sexual character."[16] This does not mean that improper sexual intimacy was the "original sin," but that sex can be steeped in egocentrism and exploitation. On the Protestant side Reinhold Niebuhr understood sin primarily as pride, but also appreciated the "Hellenistic side of Christianity" that regarded sin "as basically lust and sensuality." Since "the instincts of sex are particularly effective tools for both the assertion of the self and the flight from the self," the Hellenistic insight remains useful:

> While it must be admitted that Christian thought on sex has frequently been unduly morbid and that dualistic forms of Christianity have regarded sex as evil of itself, there are nevertheless profound insights into the problem of sex in the Christian interpretations of sin, which modern thought has missed completely.[17]

The myth of the human Fall in Genesis 3, if stripped of its misogynist interpretations, conveys that physical intimacy can be the scene of harms. The sex impulse can be an instrument of compensation or an avenue of escape. To be sure, sexual intimacy as such is good, but a sinful element has been present since the Fall. Adam and Eve, according to the narrative, covered their genitals in the aftermath of first sin. The Fall myth is not taken here literally, but metaphorically and existentially.

Kierkegaard was the major modern theologian to give a sexual interpretation of the Fall. I refer to Kierkegaard because, although he is uncritical of misogyny, I think a fair reading of his texts indicates that he is concerned with the misuse of sex equally by men and women, and his views provide a perspective that anyone can consider seriously.[10] His *The Concept of Anxiety,* published in 1844, has deep roots in the complex life of its author. His views are filled with insights that force a creative and critical appraisal of our culturally formed flight from sexual restraint. His view of the Fall is especially significant for this purpose since he finds in it a balance of spiritual pride and misused sexuality.

Kierkegaard affirms that "sensuousness in innocence is not sinfulness." He did not seek to "annihilate" the sexual, but to suggest spiritual qualifications or maturities that would afford it innocence, a qualification achieved by passing through a stage of forgetfulness, or of introducing the sexual as driven or shaped by the spirit:

> The realization of this is the victory of love in a person in whom the spirit is so victorious that the sexual is forgotten, and recollected only in forgetfulness. When this is done, sensuousness is transfigured in spirit and anxiety is driven out.[19]

Kierkegaard affirms spirit as the locus of unity of the self, and affirms sensuality insofar as it does not interfere with our recognition of spirit as that locus.

Kierkegaard is critical of the simplistic interpretation of the Fall that posits the exclusionary love of self alone as the cause of sin, because "it is by sin and in sin that selfishness comes into being." Moreover, such an interpretation "gives us no knowledge of the significance of the sexual." To reduce sin to selfishness is to define the human fault "too pneumatically, and it is not adequately observed that by being introduced, sin posits just as much a sensuous as a spiritual consequence."[20] It is difficult to discern how literally Kierkegaard takes the Fall narrative, but however he may have understood it, for him the cause of original sin is not only spiritual pride and selfishness but the misuse of sex.

As an alternative explanation of how sin both came about and comes about, Kierkegaard offers the notion of sexual seduction. Specifically, Adam and Eve are sexually intimate without spiritual qualification, and this immature intimacy is the Fall.[21] As a result, "After sin came into the world, and every time sin comes into the world, sensuousness becomes sinfulness." The effort of Christian moral catechesis has been, in response to the Fall, "to bring the spirit further,"[22] in order that sexual intimacy might become the pure good that it was meant to be.

Kierkegaard's interpretation of the Fall is not one foreign to early Christianity, as the work of Elaine Pagels indicates. Pagels points out that the Fall narrative was the primary means for defending basic values among the Christians.[23] She describes the story of Thecla (thought to be a contemporary of Paul), "the lovely young virgin who renounced a lucrative marriage which her mother had arranged, cut off her hair and dressed in men's cloths, and ran off to join the movement that Jesus and Paul had initiated." Thecla's story was a celebration of someone who "resisted family pressure, social ostracism, rape, torture, and even execution" in order to be a celibate evangelist.[24] Such religious conversions "aroused pagan relatives to outrage" and led to terrible accusations against the sect of Christianity.

Sexual restraint by both men and women, grounded in statements attributed to Jesus and Paul, was viewed as a form of indemnification for, or reversal of, the Fall. Pagels writes that stories such as Thecla's were used by preachers to persuade listeners to "undo the sin of Adam and Eve" through chaste celibacy.[25] By reversing the acts of Adam and Eve through chaste celibacy, the convert could contribute to the process of spiritual restoration, although such restoration would not fully come in this world, nor be even partially possible without grace.

Pagels explains that many Christians living a generation or more after Paul sought to soften the doctrine of sexual sin and indemnification. Clement of Alexandria, for instance, emphasized that sexual intercourse was not sinful but a part of God's "good" creation.[26] This was also a response to earlier theologians who argued that Satan invented sexual intercourse. As a part of this response, Clement and others contended that the act of original sin was disobedience to God's command. Pagels, however, adds this:

> Yet even Clement and his contemporary Bishop Irenaeus of Lyons, although eager to exempt sexual desire from primary

blame for the fall, admit that, as they imagined it, "man's first disobedience" and the fall did, in fact, take *sexual form*. Clement carefully explains that the disobedience of Adam and Eve involved not what they did, but how they did it. As Clement imagines the scene, Adam and Eve, like impatient adolescents, *rushed* into sexual union before they had their Father's blessing.[27]

They were "seduced by deceit" and, according to Irenaeus, covered their sexual parts with leaves to punish the organs that led them into sin. Thus even the more revisionist theologians living a century after Paul's death connected the Fall, which they took literally, with sex.[28] We need not accept all their conclusions, but the attention to sex as one area of human sin is worth some attention, since in modernity we seem to ignore this.

Recent Religious Ethics: Nelson and Meilaender

A significant debate has emerged in recent years regarding the extent to which religious ethics should take into account the persistence of harm and disloyalty in the sphere of sex. James B. Nelson published his highly influential *Embodiment* in 1978. It is in many respects a great book because of its affirmation of the goodness of the body. Gilbert Meilaender, in asking what remains today of Christian sexual ethics, points to Nelson's book as a widely noted, "usually applauded" touchstone that "faithfully reflects the present state of much Christian talk about sexuality and marriage."[29] But Meilaender is critical of Nelson and makes some useful points, even if some might think he does not account for the full corpus of Nelson's writings.

Nelson emphasizes that Christ was "the Word made flesh," and from this Nelson sees "the body as instrument of communion," and not merely as "physical substructure." He considers sexual desire essential to the communion between God, self, and other, so that the absence of sexual expression invites "self-destruction": "Deprived of eros, the body can become the champion of thanatos." To deny bodily *eros* "is the root experience of sin." Nelson argues that sexuality is the intrinsic center of the human relationship with God and views erotic experience "as a basic key to the eternal." He asserts that "our sexuality is a sacramental means for the love of God" and that organic "urges" of a sexual nature are central to the quest for communion with God.[30]

To his credit, Nelson attacks the repression of sexuality, and he does insist on a bond between sex and love. But, Meilaender suggests, Nelson forgets that "nature and spirit have quarreled within the human person," so that disorder and rebellion are injected into our "body-selves." Meilaender adds that the dual nature of the human self, spirit and body, is left in disharmony by sin. While Nelson does indeed have some notion of the harmony that all persons would like, the reality is that the self-transcending self (spirit) and the body (nature) are often in conflict, and that "on some occasions the body may in fact be a dangerous force in need of stern control."[31] Meilaender concludes that the self is less redeemed than Nelson supposes. In defense of Nelson, I must indicate that in his later work he does deal with sin insofar as he is concerned with the abuse of power, and with the masculine genitalization of sex that ignores spiritual intimacy.[32]

Meilaender points to another questionable departure from tradition in Nelson's argument that marital fidelity is fully consistent with nonexclusive sexual intimacies, at least in some cases.[33] This is a departure from the meaning of marital indissolubility as fidelity both in body and in spirit. I agree that Nelson does not seem to deal fully with the painful and harmful ruptures that lie in sexual infidelity, and the destructive implications of this familial dissolution for children.

Writing in 1968, a decade before Nelson, another Protestant, Daniel Day Williams, worked out a more realistic ethic, and one that I prefer. While Williams, like Nelson, acknowledges the place of sex in the human experience of communication and rejects morbid attitudes toward sexuality, he stresses more than Nelson that "the sexual life participates in the realm of freedom, in both sin and grace." Williams writes of "hurts given and received," of the tragedy of broken families and violence, and thus of "an enormous amount of silent suffering which people bear in relation to sex." He warns that however much sexual intimacy can be creative, "we have to speak of sex, as of every aspect of human life, in a double way, from the standpoint of essential created goodness, and the distortion produced by sin. In all life and love we find both aspects." Williams thus encourages self-restraint "for the sake of love." He concludes,

> Sexual obsession seems joined with a loss of true self-possession. The rules of monogamy, the proscription of sexual intercourse outside marriage, the traditional rules of sexual restraint, are important for the Christian style of life. They are the guidelines which have protected precious human relationships against willful corruption.[34]

One need not have struggled through the revolutionary sixties to recognize that unrestraint harms love. Kant was right to claim that in the domain of sexual intimacy the reduction of human beings to mere objects can occur.

Envoi

I have earlier defined love as solicitude, manifest in joy, compassion, loyalty, and respect. Sexual desire can be coupled with love, but love exists in various forms where sex is considered inappropriate, e.g., parental love, filial love, and sibling love. Sexual desire is never in and of itself love. Thus, the current language of "having sex" that seems to have replaced "making love" is, however libertine, at least honest. It does not try to disguise desire and heat with the linguistic trappings of love and heart.

In contrast, I advocate a recovery of the ethics of sex that takes love and commitment seriously. This is because there is a sacredness and profound religious meaning in conjugal love that deserves affirmation. The body and sex have sanctity because they are the instruments of the order of marriage. The traditional Christian notion of the sanctity of the human body has roots in Judaism. We have lost a sense of the sanctity of the body. Our culture inculcates an extreme on sexual expression; there is precious little room for youthful innocence, or for refusal of physical intimacy. To heal our condition an ethical theory may be necessary, but theory alone is likely to be insufficient; cultural *metanoia* is required, and that no theory can give. It is not barbarous superstition to suggest that the body should be honored as the seat of a higher principle.

The Jewish and Christian solution to the ethics of sex is marriage, which constitutes the building of God's image. Gerhard von Rad captured this central thread of religious insight in commenting on Genesis: "By God's will, man was not created alone, but designated for the 'thou' of the other sex. The idea of man finds its full meaning not in the male alone but in man and woman."[35] Marriage is a participation in the mystery of God's creation ("Be fruitful, multiply, and take dominion," Gn. 1:28), an empowerment for a spouse to complete his or her nature, and a reflection of the fatherly-motherly nature of dyadic theism. It is the completion and the sanctification of creation. With the full corrections to patriarchy in place, this basic theological idea remains viable.[36]

The unambiguous Jewish affirmation of sex in marriage is instructive for Christianity. Even when Martin Luther asserts, "But we are exactly as he created us: I a man and you a woman," and that God's "excellent handiwork" should not be despised, he nevertheless adds that "intercourse is never without sin," however much God forgives it since it is the only way to achieve the blessing of marriage and procreation.[37] Luther thus retains some of the early patristic conception of sex as negative, although he resolves the tension within marriage on the basis of a blanket forgiveness rather than by an appeal for celibacy and a higher vocation. Yet viewed more creatively, Luther's assertion that "intercourse is never without sin" exhorts us to a self-critical insight that sex even within marriage can fall into oppression because sin remains present.

The ideal of marriage in the image of God is clearly theologically driven. Human beings, like the chaos out of which God created order in Genesis 1, are capable of various sexual interactions from polygamy to same-sex relations and intercourse with nonhuman animals. There may be genetic predeterminants of homosexuality in many cases, and this implies that the behavior is largely inevitable rather than cause for accusation or social intolerance.

But Judaism and Christianity claim only that the ideal of God, the ordering from above of the chaos below, remains marriage between husband and wife and the experience of parenthood. No one would question that procreation and childrearing are uniquely possible and suitable for marriage between the committed man and woman. From the perspective of virtue and moral development, for most people the transition to parenthood and parental love signals a huge change that is pure gain, the topic of the next chapter.

4

Parental
Love

*Love as the quintessence of the character of God is not
established by argument, but taken for granted. It may be
regarded as axiomatic in the faith of prophetic religion. On the
only occasion on which Jesus makes the matter a subject for
argument he declares, "If ye then, being evil, know how to give
good gifts unto your children, how much more shall your
Father which is in heaven give good things to them that ask
him? [Mt. 7:11]." This passage is significant because Jesus,
true to the insights of prophetic religion, not only discovers
symbols of the character of God in man's mundane existence,
but also because he sees this symbol of God's love among
"evil" and not among imperfect men.*
    REINHOLD NIEBUHR, *An Interpretation of Christian Ethics*

*Making a child is a moral act. Obviously it obligates the parents
to the child. But it also obligates the parents to the community.*
    AMITAI ETZIONI, *The Spirit of Community*

This chapter flows from the previous ones, building on
dyadic theism but moving from the conjugal to the
parental manifestation of love. I presuppose that male familial dominance and oppression of women is unacceptable, as is
sexist bias in employment and society at large; that directly caring

parental love is as much the vocation of fathers as mothers; and that parents should give primacy to parental commitments. Commitment to "family values" must not mean the loss of women's rights in any spheres of life, or the license to mistreat or abuse children without fear of legal intervention. Thus the movement to define a new ethic of the family, the new familialism.

Why give such positive attention to parental love when there are evils perpetrated in its name? The broad arguments against parental love include the temptation of parents to play savior, wielding inordinate power to "protect" others, denying initiative and autonomy, or establishing unhealthy dependencies. Since these sorts of criticisms are partly valid we must be cautious about parental love. Sallie McFague argues, after a series of warnings about the potential oppression inherent in the parental metaphor, "Nevertheless, in spite of these qualifications, the maternal metaphor is so powerful and so right for our time that we *should* use it." In an age of nuclear and ecological threat, McFague claims that a metaphor emphasizing nurture and "life as a gift" is necessary, for parental love "nurtures what it has brought into existence, and wants it to grow and be fulfilled." McFague is right that "parental love is the most powerful and intimate experience we have of giving love whose return is not calculated (though a return is appreciated): it is the gift of life as such to others."[1] But parental love is not a paradigm of all love, for it is by definition paternalistic or maternalistic rather than equalitarian. If Aristotle is right that true friendship exists between equals, then parental love is problematic for many relationships.

Yet there is much value in McFague's emphasis on the importance of parental love—certainly if it is contained within the parent-child domain. Stripped of oppressive aspects, an analogy between the parental heart of God and of good human parents for their children can and should be asserted. The parental heart puts children first; the dissolution of marriage, however good for parents, is seldom good for children, although it is justified in some circumstances. This dissolution, along with the immense problem of children having children, constitutes one of the most significant moral and theological issues of our time. The "parenting deficit" in our society is harmful to the community because it is harmful to children who come to constitute that community. As Amitai Etzioni emphasizes, "We must all live with the consequences of children who are not brought up properly, whether bad economic conditions or self-centered parents are to blame."[2]

McFague's emphasis is on parentism as a response to nuclear war and environmental harms; in contrast, I construct a moral and theological place for parental love in the family because there are innocent children whose lives are deeply harmed by fatherlessness and motherlessness. Many of these children are left incapable of ethical and constructive participation in society. This harm can overwhelm society morally, financially, politically, and socially.

One of the most significant publications on the parenting deficit and long-term damage to children as well as society is the 1991 report of the National Commission on Children, chaired by Senator John D. Rockefeller. This bipartisan commission marshalled massive empirical evidence to assert that "rising rates of divorce, out-of-wedlock childbearing, and absent parents are not just manifestations of alternative lifestyles, they are patterns of adult behavior that increase children's risk of negative consequences." Moreover, "following divorce, or when parents do not marry, many children experience not only financial hardship, but psychological and emotional injury as well." The commission calls for a "renewed commitment to children and families—to marriage, parenthood, and childhood."[3] In a balanced assessment of the parenting deficit, both "personal responsibility and moral strength among parents" and social and economic systemic shortcomings are stressed, as they should be.

That commitment to the parental vocation is a major factor shaping the future of children is beyond any reasonable doubt. As Etzioni highlights, under the same economic conditions, whether affluent or poor, and of whatever ethnic group, "one finds decent and hardworking youngsters right next to antisocial ones."[4] Or as Barbara Dafoe Whitehead states, economic, political, and technological forces affect the family for good or for ill, "but the principal source of family decline over the past three decades has been cultural." Values have come into favor that are destructive of commitment, responsibility, and sacrifice. "The family has weakened," she continues, "because, quite simply, many Americans have changed their minds." They have changed their minds about commitment to marriage and to parenthood, about being unmarried and pregnant, and about putting the needs of children first. Moreover, "many American men changed their minds about the obligations of a father and husband."[5] Fatherlessness is a massive social problem, especially for the adolescent boy left without his essential role model and moral mentor.

A vital task of ethics and theology is to provide a world view and symbol system supportive of parental love and the ethic of children first. To a significant degree, both Judaism and Christianity have provided these things in the past, but with gender injustice. A just and caring fatherhood is good for men, children, and mothers: "there is surely nothing in our natures that requires men not to be equal participants in the rearing of their children."[6]

This assertion is valid, and fathers like mothers have a unique parental function. It is wrong that some extol "family values" while insisting that women alone do the direct caring. The only parental love worthy of defending is a just love. Fathers should nurture, as Larry May and Robert Strikwerda contend, and nurturance should become "the dominant characteristic of their role as fathers."[7] Any call for parental love that is really a call only for maternal love fails the test of justice. If we set aside Jean-Jacques Rousseau's gendered ideas about the woman's role as exclusive caregiver—Rousseau incidentally sent his own children to orphanages rather than raise them himself—we quickly discover that in the seventeenth and eighteenth centuries, American colonial fathers "had primary responsibility for child care beyond the early nursing period."[8] Jonathan Edwards, James Madison, Aaron Burr, Lyman Beecher, and scores of other historical American men tutored and raised their children. John Adams and Thomas Jefferson were raised by their fathers. It was only in the early nineteenth century that exclusive mother-care became the norm, and this was because fathers began to establish places of work away from the home.[9]

Damaged Children, Damaged Society

David Popenoe, a family sociologist, asks, "How can we uphold the virtues of the nuclear family without returning to the lifestyles of the 1950s, and thereby compromise the movement of women toward full participation in the economy and in public life, and stigmatize those who are not fortunate enough to have strong nuclear families?"[10] Popenoe's concern with stigmatization is as important as his wish to retain gains for women, particularly in a modern society that offers the family little ideological or cultural support. Many of our teenage single mothers are victims of wider cultural and social-economic forces, although they are still responsible moral agents.

Even parents in nuclear families who are deeply committed to their children may not have the time for frequent parent–child interaction, because both mother and father must work in order to survive in an economy that truly burdens families. Certainly paid parental leaves, access to health care, stable jobs, and a societal commitment to the education of children are matters of justice that go far beyond the scope of familial control. Poverty creates higher divorce rates, and jobless fathers are not prone to marriage. The relation of the parenting deficit to a complex web of economic and social ills is clear. Stephanie Coontz considers the economic decline of large population segments in America and rightly thinks it simplistic to attribute all our social problems to family change.[11] Nevertheless familial decline is a very significant cultural and independent variable that can be addressed on its own terms rather than simply as a by-product of social and economic forces. It is equally simplistic to think that the parenting deficit is not an independent factor that deeply threatens the American future. There are many poor parents with the determination to be good parents.

The modern nuclear family is the remnant of the kin network of the extended family; it is the last bastion of security for the child, but it too is breaking down. And because the kin network has evaporated, caregiving requires more time and sacrifice in the nuclear family, as I will consider in chapter 6. After a lifelong study of families in Europe and the United States, Popenoe concludes: "Intact nuclear families can clearly be dysfunctional, but the weight of evidence strongly points to the generally lower quality of postnuclear families, especially single-parent families and stepfamilies."[12]

The mounting evidence is that, with exceptions, children who grow up in single-parent families do less well than those who grow up in intact nuclear families, and that this is true regardless of race, class, or sex. Of course children will do relatively well with a committed, caring, successful, and financially comfortable single mother, although the child will wonder why it has no father. The greatest suffering for children results from unmarried teenage pregnancy. In 1990 there were 4,158,212 babies born in the United States, of whom 8.7 percent (or more than one out of every twelve) were born to an unmarried teenager. 67.1 percent of teen births in 1990 were nonmarital, in contrast to 30 percent in 1970. A strong trend emerges: of total births in 1990, including all ethnic-racial groups, 28 percent were to unmarried women; of all births to African-American women 66.5 percent were to unmarried. An estimated half of white and greater than 90 percent of African-American teen mothers are unmarried. Nearly half of African-American girls will be unmarried mothers before they reach 18 years of age, and many will have more than a single child.[13] What does this mean for the future? That a very large number of children both white and black are growing up fatherless, including the vast majority of African-American children.

There are some parental tasks that fathers can do better than women, especially with respect to the attitudes and behavior of teenage boys, who require a mentoring male presence that understands what such boys must go through to mature. Female children of unmarried mothers are likely to become unmarried mothers themselves and at increasingly young ages. Male children of unmarried mothers are not likely to become responsible husbands or fathers.[14] The community, in turn, pays a monetary and social cost. Emotional incapacitation, aggressive behaviors, educational failure, relative poverty, need for psychological help, more delinquencies regardless of family income, depression, suicide, substance abuse, and nonmarital pregnancies are among the variables that increase when a child does not have the advantages of a loving mother and father sharing the often overwhelming responsibilities of parenthood. These realities are demonstrated by the longitudinal studies now available for the first time.[15]

Slightly less than 50 percent of American children can expect to spend their full childhood in an intact family, due largely to divorce and single parenting.[16] Families have become less child-centered, more focused on the value of expressive individualism than on parental commitment. And as Popenoe comments, "Parents seldom break up a relationship to benefit the children; it is to benefit themselves, that is, typically their needs for intimacy are not being met. If children had a say in such matters, the rate of family dissolution most assuredly would drop." Popenoe, echoing concerns of Robert Bellah and Christopher Lasch, sees a fundamental value conflict between individualism and familialism, and "in the current era individualism has had a remarkable run."[17] The parenting deficit in America will adversely affect the quality of national life for decades to come, unless an epic cultural transition occurs along with social and economic supports to sustain it.

Criticisms of Parental Love

Parental love has been subjected to a series of important criticisms when applied analogously by rulers to society at large. My interest in such love is strictly linked with the extended or nuclear family. Much of Enlightenment Anglo-American political thought emerged from John Locke's necessary refutation of Sir Robert Filmer's patriarchalism, i.e., of fatherhood writ large so as to justify the absolute power of kings.[18] In *Patriarcha,* Filmer develops a patriarchal doctrine of fatherhood in order to defeat the movement toward equality and liberty.[19] Drawing on the Genesis account and

emphasizing God's creation of one man as father of all, Filmer concludes that all children must be subject to their fathers, and extrap-
olates this into a political theory of the divine right of kings.
Locke's refutation of Filmer was pure gain for equality and liberty.

A significant modern philosophical repudiation of Filmer-like
ideas is that of Michael A. Slote, who writes that "not long ago"
the idea that "we are all God's children" and that God has done for
us what parents do for their children seemed attractive. Indeed,
Slote argues that the analogy between God's creation and parental
love has served as a manipulative religious device to ensure filial
piety, obedience, and political absolutism while denying autonomy.[20] To some degree, Slote is correct.

But I remain appreciative of a spiritual tradition in Roman
Catholicism that does apply parental love to the world. For example, as Ivone Gebara notes, a rich tradition of "spiritual motherhood" exists among the Catholic women religious. Gebara articulates a motherhood that leaps over institutional walls, one that can
"beget though barren," characterized by "wise women whose
close connection with life's realities enables them to listen to, feel
for, advise and help those (of both sexes) who come to them."
Gebara continues: "These women—widows, married, single parents, with few or numerous dependents—exercise a 'spiritual
motherhood' among the people without giving their daily gift of
life, their begetting of the Spirit, this or any other name."[21]

Thus, all valid suspicions considered, I think that McFague has
articulated a central religious intuition when she writes that the
image of God is mother-father-parental love. The moral ideal she
suggests is to "see ourselves as universal parents, as profoundly desiring not our own lives to go on forever but the lives of others to
come into being." Our essential task is to "universalize parenthood."[22] McFague understands the criticisms of parental love, and
she is clearly *not* suggesting that our relations with others be mod-
eled after the inequalities and power asymmetries of parent-child
relations. She has in mind the expression of parental love that
would apply to adult children, replete with freedom and equality.

A further criticism of parental love is that daughters and

daughters-in-law have been manipulated or coerced by some parents into roles as filial caregivers. Given the pervasiveness of coerced filial care, feminist suspicions seem valid. The feminist is critical of the ideal of selfless mother love as a patriarchal imposition that can violate the integrity of women.[23] Jeffner Allen, in an antinatalist essay entitled "Motherhood: The Annihilation of Women," contends that "motherhood is dangerous to women because it continues the structure within which females must be women and mothers and conversely, because it denies to females the creation of a subjectivity and world that is open and free."[24] In some cases, no doubt, motherhood is dangerous for the mother. However, my assumption is that were most mothers asked whether motherhood has "annihilated" them, they would find the question extreme and even peculiar.

Margaret Farley rightly points out that at times, parents can violate the respect that I have included as an expression of any genuine love: "A father or a mother, for example, may love a child primarily as a duplication of or a projection of themselves. In this love they may be extremely attentive to the child, meeting his every wish, but pushing him to a future that will ultimately be destructive to him."[25] Parental love must respect the freedom of the child within reasonable limits, especially as he or she matures (an issue addressed in the next chapter). But it is important to balance Farley's concern with Stanley Hauerwas's argument that parents need the courage to raise their children with "a moral role that gives them a status in the community."[26] The absence of such a role results in anomie, which has its costs in rootlessness and the fierce struggle to find meaning in a wider society that provides nothing other than the morally minimal "do no harm" principle and the requirement of economic success. Hauerwas believes that parents should be willing to raise children into a meaningful community. Children need authority-in-love as well as rights.

Parental love is also a potentially too exclusive affection. Against such concerns, the philosopher John Benson takes the position that wider affections find their root in particular ones: "My concern for other people begins with natural affections towards kin, friends, and colleagues and so on, and is extended by recognizing other human beings as potential reciprocating objects of the same affections." He continues, "This modification and spreading of particular affections may approach in its effects but is quite different in principle from an impartial concern which attempts to eliminate as irrelevant the actual relationships in which the agent stands and the moral claims they generate." Benson cautions against attempts to eliminate partial affections, since "it may remove the source of all affections."[27] Yet Benson has failed to convince many moral philosophers, because he never explains how this movement from the particular to the universal occurs. Likewise, many religious ethicists will reject the centrality of parental love unless it can be shown convincingly that parental love can be freed from a hermetic tendency.

Parental love is one of the great altruistic emotions, once given its due by Adam Smith and David Hume but dethroned by the Kantian view that discredits the emotions as transitory, changeable, and capricious, replacing them with supposedly more reliable rational motives. But parental love is not just a mood of warm feelings; it is a sustained emotional tendency toward the good of another. Transitory moods can be distinguished from genuine love. It is precisely in parental love that the altruistic emotions can develop and find affirmation consistent with the child's good. This altruism can then be applied in various nonparental relations, such as friendship or even love for the stranger, consistent with equality and freedom.

On Human Parental Love *in Imagine Dei*

Conceiving God as the Mother-Father of all creation makes the parental heart of good mothers and fathers a point of human resonance with the heart of God. My interest is in the solicitous heart that we expect of ordinary parents toward their children, and the limited but nevertheless profound analogy between this human experience and the heart of God. As Daniel Day Williams suggested, "We have seen in our study of the biblical view of love that if we say human experience throws no light on the meaning of the divine love, we are departing from the biblical mode of speaking about God."[28]

While Judaism and Christianity are in many respects discontinuous, it is proper to speak of a Judeo-Christian tradition regarding the idea of parental love as following a pattern of divine creation. The Jewish *chesed* or "steadfast love" is most frequently captured in the Hebrew Bible by the intimate familial love of parent for child. Paul Ramsey articulates the Christian continuation of such:

> Of course, we cannot see into the mystery of how God's love created the world. . . . Nevertheless, we procreate new beings like ourselves in the midst of our love for one another, and in this there is a trace of the original mystery by which God created the world.[29]

Judeo-Christian thought elevates to the sanctity of divine image that steadfast love which fuses parental creation and committed love.

Every natural theology presumes that something of the character of the creator can be gleaned from creation. Can a woman and man bringing a child into the world amidst steadfast love be *in imagine Dei?* Paul wrote that God's attributes "have been visible, ever since the world began, to the eye of reason, in the things he has made" (Rom. 1:20). According to Genesis, man and woman together are the image of God. Brunner writes of the "divine pedagogy of creation."[30] Building on the symbolic importance of threeness, I noted in a previous chapter that Brunner refers to the communion between mother, father, and child as "the trinity of being we call the human structure of existence."[31]

A natural theology of parental love is seldom made explicit. One articulation is found in John Burnaby's epilogue to *Amor Dei.* Burnaby describes the life of the child as beginning with complete dependence on parental love, from which he or she learns to be "a *causa efficiens*" of love. Burnaby continues:

> If we now attempt to trace a corresponding pattern in the love which is God's own nature, it will be in the faith common to St. Augustine and St. Thomas, that His invisible

things are understood through the things that are made, that there is a relation not of identity but of analogy, between the natural and the supernatural, between the changing and the changeless Good.[32]

It is God's parental love that is reflected in the human heart; so also, it is the love of a parent that teaches a child what love is.

Jesus of Nazareth appealed often to the parental metaphor in describing the nature of God and God's kingdom. Even sinful people give good gifts to their children (Mt. 7:11). Of the kingdom of Heaven, these words are attributed to Jesus: "There was a king who prepared a feast for his son's wedding" (Mt. 22:1–2). In his frustration over rejection, the Gospel of Matthew depicts Jesus in naturalistic and parental terms: "O Jerusalem, Jerusalem, the city that murders the prophets and stones the messengers sent to her! How often I have longed to gather your children, as a hen gathers her brood under her wings, but you would not let me" (Mt. 23:37). The parable of the Prodigal Son might well better be entitled the Parable of the Merciful Father.

With appropriate removal of language reflective of patriarchy, these verses are useful signposts: parental love tells us something about God's heart. It is noteworthy that the image of a hen gathering her brood is feminine. Moreover, as Marie-Theres Wacker states, the eleventh chapter of Hosea, often "celebrated by biblical scholars as the song of God the Father's love for Israel," in fact does not use the word "father." Indeed, the word "father" occurs sparingly in the Hebrew Bible. The parental activities in Hosea used to describe God are "a mother's everyday activities."[33] So when considering the analogy between God and the human parental heart, patriarchal language can be avoided consistent with scripture.

Through the experience of parental love one begins to understand God's desire for reunion with all humanity. If human parents suffer over their children, then how much more must God? Indeed, for those who accept the parental analogy between human and God, a process theism in which God suffers in *pathos* from the waywardness of all human beings seems inevitable. It becomes imperative to universalize love so that all people might be encouraged to return to God.[34] There is no other solution to divine *pathos*. And it is this sense of divine *pathos* that Abraham Heschel thought defined the lives of the Hebrew prophets.[35] I acknowledge that parental love should be haunted by the requirement of universal love. But a parental love prophetically sensitive to divine *pathos* does not strain against the requirement of universal love; rather, it engenders such love, and makes "benevolence to being in general" possible.

The Omission of Parental Love from Ethics

Theological ethicists have not given parental love due attention. The emphasis on love for strangers encourages commitments beyond the field of familial relations. Love for strangers is immensely important, but when love for the stranger obscures the moral significance of parental love, there is cause for criticism. In fact, parental love is quite compatible with love for strangers. This is because parents typically display love for children as soon as they are born, before the child's attributes and character have developed. Parental love is thus at least in part the love of bestowal unable to provide reasons of appraisal, and it often is remarkably unconditional and steadfast even when children and adult children manifest neither virtues nor talents. Such love is not unlike love for the stranger or even for the enemy, features of Christian love, since parental love is in many cases not conditional on performances and reciprocity. It is plausible that insofar as Christian ethics assumes God's universal love despite countless human misdeeds, it is because God is parent of us all, and therefore cannot ultimately exclude any of us.

Parental love was called *storge* by the Greeks, referring to affection generally but more especially to that of parents to offspring.[36] I do not say that parental love is as manifest as I think it should be. Psychiatrist Willard Gaylin writes, "Love is not to be equated with the genetic bonding of animals—it is less and more. It is surely less immutable, as is evident from the number of neglecting parents and even more so from the number of barbaric parents who beat and batter their children."[37] Because parental love can be withheld or negated, there is good reason to renew emphasis on the religious images and symbols that encourage parents to love their children. This is a major responsibility of our religious institutions, which they must meet if they are to remain faithful to their traditions.[38] Robert Jay Lifton, in his psychohistories of Nazi doctors, points out repeatedly that the origins of cruelty and inhumanity characteristic of those persons who engage in radical evil lies often in the fact that they received inadequate parental love, or were abused by parents.[39] Many psychiatrists argue that a person's future self-esteem is in large part formed by the amount of love received from parents in approximately the first eighteen months of life. This is why parental love is so vital for society.

Much of the love in our world is grounded in parenthood; and the love learned within the crucible of the parent–child relation can encompass others, albeit stripped of paternalist and maternalist elements fitting only for those who are not adults, as a pebble cast into water creates ripples that move outward. On the other hand, parental love can become narrow and even obsessive, precluding this expansive movement. Parental love permeated by the narratives of religious traditions that view all human beings as children of God does not deserve the suspicions that might apply to *storge* in the absence of such narratives.

By love I mean a loyal commitment to the psychophysical and spiritual well-being of the beloved consistent with freedom. Purvis sees love in her experience of motherhood: "While there may be mothers who experience agape more fully with their spouses or friends, the most sustained and trustworthy embodiment of agape in my life is my experience of being a mother to my two sons."[40] In emphasizing parental love, I have moved away from the starting point of Jonathan Edwards's "love for being in general," and from his doubts about natural affections while directly caring for his own children. In 1755, Edwards wrote:

> That kind of affection which is exercised one towards another
> in natural relation, particularly the love of parents to their

children, called natural affection, is by many referred to instinct. I have already considered this sort of love as an affection that arises from self-love: and in that view, have shown that it cannot be of the nature of true virtue.[41]

The "private affection" to children falls short of a "universal benevolence to being in general," and is therefore for Edwards suspect. He did not think that love can expand from the one to the many, given the tendency of love for those near and dear to exclude those distant and unknown.

But I consider parental love to be one locus from which love for the stranger can emerge, although I have already indicated that this is because of the moral transformation of the agent toward responsibility and care, not because I think parentalism (paternalism or maternalism) should be applicable to most human relationships. This moral transformation occurs deeply in the particular context of parental love. Virginia Held advocates that we pay more attention to particular moral domains: "Moral theories must pay attention to the neglected realm of particular others in actual contexts."[42] She considers particular and preferential relations benign, as opportunities to develop the social affections that make concern for the stranger possible. In arguing for universal benevolence, she adamantly refuses to think of universality in the typical way:

> Particular others can, I think, be actual starving children in Africa with whom one feels empathy or even the anticipated children of future generations, not just those we are close to in any traditional context of family, neighbors, or friends. But particular others are still not "all rational beings," or "the greatest number."[43]

Held argues, as I see it, that whatever universal benevolence we are able to achieve is rooted in the learned empathy that comes with relations to those others near at hand. Moreover, there can be no commitment to human beings as such, abstractly considered, but only to particular others. But I address the "order of love" more fully in chapter 8.

The ethical importance of parental love is not emphasized, argues Sara Ruddick, because men are writing the major treatises in philosophical ethics. All moral thinking, she contends, is rooted in and shaped by the practices in which people engage. Men have traditionally been enmeshed in the marketplace, or other activities that remove them from direct caring for children. Ruddick focuses on mothering, a practice open to both women and men for which women have been primarily responsible, and from which arises a "maternal thinking." Moral thought "does not transcend its social origins," she writes, and there is no "truth from a transcendental perspective, that is, from no perspective at all." Maternal practice entails "taking on the responsibility of child care" in the most direct everyday sense from feeding to diapering. While "men can be mothers," fathers historically "are meant to provide material support for child care and to defend mothers and their children from external threat."[44] Feminist ethics thus makes an important contribution to the foundations of moral philosophy.[45] That in modern society the direct caring for children is as much the duty of fathers as mothers seems self-evident.

On the basis of this feminist critique of modern ethical theories, we are led to ask an essential question: Where should our ethical reflection begin? We should begin with reflection on care and love, but to take love as universal is to disregard particulars. We seldom achieve universal love without first struggling to love those particular persons who are entrusted to us by providence and proximity. Insofar as theology and theological ethics pattern themselves on philosophy, the centrality of a loving parental God as the paradigm of the moral life has been ignored. I thus have been led to see the value of some feminist philosophical and theological ethics as a corrective.

Nonfeminist Theological Ethics

It would be an error to suggest that all nonfeminists omit a consideration of love. James M. Gustafson's powerful and striking call for a renewed attention to familial relations was quoted in the introductory chapter of this book. The transition that Gustafson favors is evident in the work of Joseph L. Allen, who focuses on two types of covenant relationships. His "inclusive covenant" embraces "all of humanity," while the "special covenant" includes "small, intimate, primary-group relationships such as a family." "Our moral responsibilities," writes Allen, "are heavily and consciously shaped by our special covenants." Moreover, "our very humanness is thoroughly interwoven with all our special relationships."[46] The movement toward symmetry between the familial domain and that of strangers is to be lauded. Allen stresses that the domain of "special covenant" is as important as that of "inclusive covenant."

Another recent response to the omission of the familial domain and parental love is that of Norman A. Geisler. He argues that parents begin the life of *agape* by caring for their children, and then love is "to move out to their other relatives in need." Ultimately, love is like a "pebble cast into water," its initial point of contact being the family from which "the waves must move out as far as possible."[47]

In the Roman Catholic tradition, there are profound resources on parental love that should be recovered. In general, Catholic ethics has maintained the Augustinian-Thomistic readiness to interpret special relations more positively than have some Protestant ethicists. In a remarkable but overlooked French study on love, Louis Colin refers to the child as "at the confluence of two hearts, of two beings who, mingling and merging their tenderness, pour it out afterwards on this little being." He adds:

> Of all the human affections, those of fathers and mothers seem to be the most instinctive and incoercible. The very animals have a sort of uneasy, passionate solicitude for their progeny which sometimes moves us. The Carmelite of Lisieux felt her eyes moistening at the sight of the hen warming her chicks under her wings.[48]

Catholic natural law tradition understands, argues Colin, that "it is there in the mysterious depths where a human life is being shaped, in the very womb of the woman, that maternal love is first born."

It views parental love as natural and at the same time as "a participation" in God's parental being.[49]

Of course, one wants to be wary of natural law theories that impose narrow and unjust roles on women, as Okin underscores.[50] Yet Catholic social thought, with its levels of sociality and the principle of subsidiarity, does at least stick close to life as people really live it. It also sees the family as a center of habituation and virtue in the classical sense not present in modern moral philosophies. While there may be some partiarchal remnants in the 1981 papal encyclical on the family, *Familiaris Consortio* ("On the Family"), it clearly asserts that the "equal dignity and responsibility of men and women fully justifies women's access to public functions." While the maternal and family role is lauded, this can be "harmoniously" combined with professional and other roles. Throughout, the family is understood as "the first and irreplaceable school of social life, an example and stimulus for the broader community of relationships marked by respect, justice, dialogue and love."[51] It also functions to transmit basic moral values, with parents serving as models of the life based on truth, freedom, justice, and love. This encyclical is not a simple reassertion of past patriarchy, but rather a powerful evidence of progress and a "new familialism."

Parental Love under Agape

Universal love or *agape* is both continuous and discontinuous with parental love. Paternalism and maternalism are, as earlier argued, distinct from the sort of relational ethics one wants with colleagues. Yet I have also indicated some degree of sympathy with those like McFague who see value in an ethics of universal parentalism. In the final analysis, parental love is very close to paradigmatic for *agape,* so long as it respects the freedom and maturity of the other. Moreover, parental love is a crucible for moral development and the possibility of learning to love in general.

Here I disagree with Henri Bergson, who states that achieving universal love is not a question of "widening the bounds," since "between a social morality and a human morality the difference is one not of degree but of kind."[52] A crucial question for me is how one begins to "see" the universal in the particular. Is the elevation of particular love to universal love achieved by incremental change, or by a breakthrough (*metanoiai*), the work of a higher power—God's cooperant grace? Is there a "leap" from the particular to the universal like the eidetic reduction in phenomenology? These are extremely difficult questions that I have only approached here. Nevertheless, a goal of religious life is for the universal to enter into the particular.

I have in mind something akin to Tillich's notion of the universal "cutting" into the particular. Among the positions of Protestant theologians, Paul Tillich's integration of *agape* and less universal forms of love is extraordinarily insightful. He rejected the either/or approach to *agape* and other loves, preferring integration instead. *Agape,* writes Tillich, "cuts" into friendship and elevates it from the "ambiguities" of self-centeredness.[53] In a set of passages well worth recalling, Tillich clarifies his approach:

> Again, *agape* does not deny the preferential love of the *philia* quality, but it purifies it from a subpersonal bondage, and it elevates the preferential love into universal love. The preferences of friendship are not negated, but they do not exclude, in a kind of aristocratic self-separation, all the others. Not everybody is a friend, but everybody is affirmed as a person.[54]

Such friendship is not aristocratic or arrogant; rather, it exhibits the qualities of humility and openness.

I would add to Tillich by replacing *philia* with *storge,* since he appears to have ignored it, and by paraphrasing:

> Again, *agape* does not deny the preferential love of the *storge* quality, but it purifies it from a subpersonal bondage, and it elevates the preferential love into universal love. The preferences of parental love are not negated, but they do not exclude, in a kind of aristocratic self-separation, all the others. Not everybody is one's child, but everybody is affirmed as such.

I would add the principles of freedom and equality to any concentric expansion of *storge* to the world. The recovery of *storge* that I suggest is partly consistent with one of the great medieval symbols of love, the pelican, which was depicted in the act of feeding its offspring, indicative of all humanity (it was not noted that at least some pelicans toss their offspring out of the nest and leave them to die in order to care for those for whom they have sufficient resources).

There are many who will never be convinced that parental love is one heuristic key into the nature of *agape*. The critic will contend that most people are strangers to me and that it is not helpful to pretend that they are in the same moral relation to me as my children are. The idea of expanding *storge,* it might be argued, underplays the tension between obligations to near relations and just treatment of the stanger and distant persons. I acknowledge that given human finitude, most people will remain strangers to me, but I am still able to cultivate a universal love inwardly and as moral intention. Practically, I can extend the ideal of parental love by asking whether the compassion and concern I show this student or colleague, consistent with their freedom and integrity, begins to approximate the level of care I hold for those near and dear. This is no trivial mental exercise, but a real point of moral self-assessment.

Filial

Love

But the first experience of loving is in loving our parents.
Because filial love begins before we have language to define it,
this first active love, so important in our lives, remains largely
unexplained, undocumented.

DANIEL MARK EPSTEIN,
Love's Compass: A Natural History of the Heart

So he set out for his father's house. But while he was still a
long way off his father saw him, and his heart went out to
him. He ran to meet him, flung his arms round him, and
kissed him.

LUKE 15:20–21

Filial love has not been a topic of much interest in ethics either in the past or recently. The relation of child to parent has fallen in the category of honor or respect, as in the first interpersonal commandment of the Decalogue: "Honor thy father and thy mother." But if a parent fails to elicit filial love, then the commandment to honor is a poor substitute. The venerable idea of honoring parents is pertinent, but as the expression of a filial love that is a response to parental love.

Parental Love Creates Filial

The love of a child for parents can only be a response to the love of parents for a child; it is the first love that a child can have and it is therefore important for the child's development that parents create the conditions under which it can be elicited. John Burnaby, in the epilogue to his classic study of love in Augustine, develops an analogy between parent-child love and the communion between God and human beings. Burnaby states that the infant and young child are reactive to external sources of gratification; "but sooner or later comes the new stage, in which memory and imagination turn the passive recipient into an active originator." The child "is no longer *only* a reaction to presented good, but also a *causa efficiens*."[1] True parental love will evoke a responsive solicitude, the gradual development of filial love; and filial love encourages sibling love, for one cannot ignore other children and still love filially.

Filial love can never be demanded, only elicited. The parent is endowed with a love of children that makes it normally a pleasure to contribute to their welfare. But the child does not have a corresponding natural love of the parent. Filial love in contrast to parental must be prompted and nurtured. Daniel Mark Epstein, in his study of "the natural history of the heart," makes this astute observation: "We are born from total darkness into a blinding light in which we cannot distinguish ourselves from mother or anything else in nature. Yet even before we recognize ourselves or our surroundings, love has been working on us for some time." Epstein reflects as far back as he can on his own childhood, and concludes what most fortunate people would agree to: "The first experience of love is being loved, by our parents." Early mother-love in particular elicits the initial return of love from the child, Epstein suggests. "As I got older," he concludes, "I became more conscious of my feelings, but the basic emotion of filial love did not change after childhood."[2]

The natural history of the heart in filial love is the beginning of much human solicitude, for this is where love is first learned in most cases. It is difficult to imagine much moral idealism in a world lacking such solicitude, one in which young children grew up scorned, neglected, and abused. This is one reason why society has a communitarian interest in responsible parenting. While there are some weaknesses in Nel Noddings's study of caring, she makes an argument that is surely valid: a foundation for later moral development is the experience of being cared for as an infant and young child.[3] These earliest memories are of a caring mother, for "whatever she does, she conveys to the cared-for that she cares."[4] Few children can grow up to respect the principle "Do no harm" if they have no solicitude for others, and without them having the deep memory of being cared for such solicitude is unlikely.

It is urgent that our culture understand this: Without the experience of parental love the child lives in resentment and anger that makes it much more difficult to love others; the more likely result of such absence of parental love is that the child will inflict wanton harms on self and others. Potential parents must then be prepared to care for the children they will bring into the world, lest a generation of children be lost to themselves and society. Adherence to all moral restraints depends on the child having a basic solicitude or care for others; a society in which parents fail to love their children is one in which a new generation will be unable to take their rightful place. It seems obvious that the attitudes and values of children are the fruit of family life: "Love breeds love, violence stimulates violence, indifference fosters indifference and apathy."[5]

The child must grow into filial love. Among the conditions for the growth of filial love are personal attention, attentive listening, and favorable responses from parents. A native capacity to love is developed in the child, and this capacity is the basis for all other loves. Innumerable psychohistories indicate that destructive lives stem in part from parental abuse or neglect, although it is possible to place too much blame on parents, as though, on some level, adult children are not ultimately responsible for their actions.[6]

Following the lead of Judaism, one of the contributions of Christianity to Western familial culture has been the importance afforded to the child. In Mark 10:14–16, Jesus indignantly rebukes his disciples for preventing children from approaching him: "And he put his arms around them, laid his hands upon them, and blessed them." These passages follow immediately after the prohibition of divorce (Mk. 10:10–12), suggesting that in this prohibition Christianity had the welfare of children as much in mind as the sanctity of conjugal love. Christianity makes a new place for children in the family, sanctioning each new life by a christening in which parents vow to provide love. The protection and nurturing of children becomes the primary value of the family. Through this the child grows into love.

Filial Freedom: Rembrandt's Prodigal Son

Even the most affective and directly loving parent is uncertain of filial response. There is no better narrative for reflecting on this point than the parable of the prodigal son (Lk. 15:11–32), and no better interpretation of the prodigal for our purposes than that of Henri J. M. Nouwen as he considers the meanings in Rembrandt's painting *The Return of the Prodigal Son.* Nouwen focuses on the hands of the father in Rembrandt's great depiction. The father emanates forgiveness upon the prodigal's return, manifesting a love that is too great for force or constraint, that gives the son freedom to reject or return love. The son had run away to a distant country and the father was powerless to prevent. Nouwen sees in this father and his relation with the son all the essentials of a constructive theology:

> Here is the God I want to believe in, a Father who, from the beginning of creation, has stretched out his arms in merciful blessing, never forcing himself on anyone, but always waiting; never letting his arms drop down in despair, but always hoping that his children will return so that he can speak words of love to them and let his tired arms rest on their shoulders. His only desire is to bless.[7]

This is a grieving, forgiving, and generous God.

Especially significant is Nouwen's insight into the hands of the father. Several art critics have commented that the left hand of the father is masculine and probably the artist's own, while the right hand is distinctively feminine.[8] So the father as Rembrandt captures him is not the great patriarch but mother as well, touching the son with masculine and feminine hands. Observing the actions of both hands in the painting, Nouwen adds: "He holds, and she caresses. He confirms and she consoles. He is, indeed, God, in whom both manhood and womanhood, fatherhood and motherhood, are fully present." There is unconditional love from a God who is "Father as well as Mother."[9] The return of the prodigal was cause for celebration after the father's long suffering. In these images Nouwen finds the analogical beginnings of a very simple but profound theology, i.e., God is to humanity as parent is to child.

An Analogical–Familial Theology

A crucial tool we bring to our interpretation of the world and of the divine is analogy. Dorothy Emmet's definition serves well:

> An analogy in its original root meaning is a proportion, and primarily a mathematical ratio, e.g., 2:4::4:X. In such a ratio, given knowledge of three terms, and the nature of the proportionate relation, the value of the fourth term can be determined. Thus analogy is the repetition of the same fundamental pattern in two different contexts.[10]

When we employ analogical reasoning we claim that a pattern obvious in one context applies in another, so analogy means "argument from parallel cases." In analogical reasoning we infer from the fact that two (or more) items share related and significant properties that they are more or less likely to share another relevant property one of them is already known to have. Two entities are analogous if the relevant aspects of one are related in such a way that they agree with or correspond to the way in which the relevant aspects of the other entity are related.

The conclusions of analogical reasoning lack the certainty of a geometric theorem. When we use "analogy" or "analogical" we refer to all those arguments that emphasize similarities between apparently dissimilar phenomena. Of these phenomena one is usually better understood than the other; what is better known is used to illuminate the less well known. Theologically, the relation of parent and child is known, and from it we illumine the relation of God to human beings. This seems absolutely central to Judaism and Christianity, for scripture is replete with familial metaphors.

Analogical thinking frequently finds expression in metaphor, allegory, and parable. Analogical thought, far from being opposed to conceptual thinking, is one means by which we form concepts of the God-human relation. Such analogical reasoning is a powerful pedagogical tool and is well suited for moral education. In Jewish and Christian thought, analogical thought based on familial-divine continuities is like the air we breathe; it is so deeply embedded in the language and traditions of a community of interpretation that the user is not always aware of its centrality.

A task of the theologian such as Nouwen is to develop analogies that may force open new horizons of interpretation. Such innovation should be highly valued as a pedagogical tool. Analogies often have a powerful effect on the listener, for people tend to remember striking analogies. New analogies expose what has not been considered and can uproot dogmatic mindsets.[11] Nevertheless, new analogies, as much as old ones, require evaluation, for an analogy can lead to evil consequences as well as good ones.

Mark Turner writes that analogy succeeds through the process of "putting pressure" on our "category clusters." All thinking is the subsumption of an object under a concept, or the categorization of an object. Powerful analogies can lead to the restructuring of our troubled assumptions about what is like what. "A deep, surprising analogy may be compelling to us in the sense that it suggests weird but powerful connections between concepts (including deeply generatively entrenched concepts)."[12] Through analogy we can cross over the normal walls of categorical domains; this process can be morally and theologically enriching.

Theological ethics consists in large part in elucidating analogies that place the imagination before a novel horizon. William F. May says: "Moral reflection attempts, at its best, a knowledgeable revisioning of the world that human practice presents. Corrective vision of this sort offers an immensely practical freedom. We cannot change our behavior unless, in some respects, our perception of the world also changes."[13] This revisioning is not a remote and abstract enterprise. Insightful comparisons are a means by which we are enabled to correct our vision or change our standpoint.

From the time human beings as children begin to think, they usually learn by finding the similar in the apparently dissimilar. They learn the meaning of "spherical" by looking at an orange, a grapefruit, and a globe of the earth. They continue to learn this way as adults, though comparisons become more complex. Practical reasoning and imperative inference require analogy because this is a basic way in which human beings think and learn. Sometimes the best an ethicist or theologian can do is to provide analogies that help us become conscious of our interpretations of the world and thereby reflect on them. The development of moral awareness, the *prise de conscience* that takes place however slowly,[14] occurs when new analogies lift people beyond the limits of their previous interpretations.

As already mentioned, Burnaby like Nouwen sees an analogy or corresponding pattern between parent–child love and the love of Jewish and Christian faiths, since according to Romans 1:20, "His invisible things are understood through the things that are made." God's grace is "everywhere prevenient," and our "deepest insight into the divine purpose shows us the will of God to unite us to Himself as children to the Father."[15] Were Burnaby writing today, one surmises he would speak of God as motherly and fatherly as does Nouwen.

Following Burnaby and the classical Catholic-Anglican assumption that something of the character of the Creator can be known from creation, I take the "natural history of love" touched on by Epstein and Noddings with theological seriousness as a suggestive opening to knowledge about God. I believe a full theology can be constructed around the profoundly simple observation that a child's first acts of loving will be the sharing of a poem, drawing, or whatever it may be with a parent who loved from the first and conveyed the secure feeling of "I am loved because I am" to the child. Of these initial acts of filial love, Erich Fromm adds, "For the first time in the child's life the idea of love is transformed from being loved into loving; into creating love."[16]

Christian love within the community of faith begins from the great scriptural affirmation "God is love." It proceeds from a Mother-Father God and elicits human filial response, from which love of others emerges. This spreading of filial love to encompass all others, since they are also God's children, is a necessary test of love for God. Thus the biblical assertion that all claims to have love for God are invalid until relations have been set straight with the neighbor. This outward tendency of true filial love for God begins within the faith community, after the injunction "This is my commandment: love one another as I have loved you" (Jn. 15:12); it includes love toward the neighbor, who is everyone, after the injunction "love your neighbor as yourself" (Lk. 10:27); it even encompasses love toward enemies, following the command "Love your enemies and pray for your persecutors" (Mt. 5:44). But all love for friends in faith, for the neighbor in general, and for the persecutor follows directly as an outgrowth of filial love for God. A chief expression of such love for others is, following Augustine, encouraging them to realize that God exists, that God is love, and that filial love for God is the ontological fulfillment of the human person.

The critic may contend that the analogy of mysterious divine-human love to parent-child love is anthropomorphic, and that such an analogy can never be verified. The analogical theology of Anglicanism and Catholicism is an obvious contrast to much Protestant thinking. Karl Barth powerfully attacked the *analogia entis,* and from Kant onward the premises of the venerable old natural theology have been flailed. Yet it is no less reasonable to draw the analogies I am suggesting than to scorn them. Moreover, to defer again to Daniel Day Williams, the Hebrew Bible as well as the New Testament are replete with theological analogies to parent-child love.[17] Jesus himself, whether in the parable of the Prodigal Son or in dozens of other passing allusions, seems to have drawn very deeply on the analogy to familial loves and related common experiences.

My view is that creative analogies to a loving Mother-Father God, such as the one Nouwen so beautifully develops from Rembrandt, function to strengthen the loving inclinations of parents that elicit filial love. Parental love is rarely as consistent or reliable as we wish it were. The reality of child abuse and the need for child protection laws indicates that parental love can erode.[18] While we cannot always predict the effects of maltreatment, children "most often suffer multiple damage, and individual susceptibilities to harm differ."[19] Insofar as a functionalist notion of religion appreciates the power of symbol to affect culture, the image of a dyadic Mother-Father God may have some value for the encouraging of parental love from generation to generation.

The Absence of Filial Love

No mother or father who has (1) inflicted significant harms on their child, (2) left unfulfilled the basic responsibilities of parenting consistent with social context, or (3) been devoid of any direct affective affirmation of the child should expect filial love. Filial love is the child of parental love. If one additional commandment could be added to the Decalogue, "Love thy children" would be a prime candidate. That the Decalogue omits a commandment to love and honor one's children is unfortunate, since in various instances it appears that parental love requires such encouragement. The authoritarian notion that parents have a right to respect or to love simply because they are parents is as erroneous as it is desperate.

One of the mainstays of Western morality is that adult children who have benefited from loving and responsible parents are obligated to care for the latter. Yet when parents have been irresponsible and uncaring, filial love and the related sense of obligation are in serious doubt. An adequate discussion of filial love cannot be concerned only with the vast majority of parents who provide their children with the basic requirements of a good upbringing as the conventions of a given society define this, coupled with a reasonably enduring loving disposition. There are clear failures in parental loving that must not be glossed over. Indeed, part of my intent here is to develop a sacred canopy of meanings for parental love so that failures might be prevented. Parental love is, of course, much more than the provision of external necessities. By virtue of their having procreated children, parents have a primary obligation to provide love and to respond to significant needs. Giving their time and being personally present is as important as anything else.

Moreover, parental love should be reasonably free from self-interested motives. The parents who bring children into the world as social insurance have not infrequently forced daughters to assume lives of filial servitude.[20] Often, when we speak of filial love and responsibility as it has existed in the past, this is merely a euphemism for what a daughter supposedly owes her parents on the mere grounds that it was they who brought her into the world. D. Lydia Bronte points out that several decades ago in rural Arkansas, when she grew up as a young girl, some parents practiced a form of familial slavery. A daughter would sometimes be viewed as "property" by her parents, and by virtue of her gender was forced to remain unmarried and at home as a permanent caretaker. Some daughters resigned themselves to this fate, while others rebelled and married against parental wishes; some of these latter were driven to emotional breakdowns "by the resulting anger and vindictiveness of the disappointed parents."[21] Whether this practice continues, I do not know. That it has existed underscores the ambiguity of filial morality from the viewpoint of women. To strip anyone of basic human rights to movement and marriage in order to ensure that filial obligations are met is to undercut the foundation of love upon which such obligations themselves should rest.

Jewish and Christian traditions may go too far in emphasis on filial piety akin to religious awe. "Each person," we are told, "shall revere his mother and father" (Lv. 19:12). In a passage that follows, the child is to "rise up and respect the presence of an old man" just as one would rise up before God (Lv. 19:32). The commandment to honor parents itself lies uncomfortably close to those in the Decalogue that prescribe religious worship. The *Mekilta de-Rabbi*

Ishmael, a rabbinic commentary on Exodus, reads as follows: "The honoring of one's father and mother is very dear in the sight of Him by whose word the world came into being. For He declared honoring them to be equal to honoring Him, fearing them equal to fearing Him, and cursing them equal to cursing Him."[22] Surely filial piety has dangers, for it implies that obligations are unlimited. One can easily sympathize with the feminist concern over patriarchal manipulation of filial morality, and with Michael A. Slote's thesis, referred to in the previous chapter, that submission to parental authority can only be undercut when the illusions of a religion that worships the divine father are exposed.[23]

On a more apologetic note, if in Jewish and Christian tradition the authority of parents is an image of God's authority, there can still be spiritual and legal remedies for the abuse of this authority. It is noteworthy that the movement for the rights of children has emerged on Western soil nurtured by Judaism and Christianity. Such a movement has not emerged, however, in the pan-Confucianism of Asia, where filial piety is more absolute. Christianity is emphatic about the worth of the child, and Jesus chided his disciples for keeping children from him.

Filial Love and Reciprocity

Reciprocity means that person A acts in a certain way expecting person B to respond in a certain way. If B fails to respond, then he or she is dubbed ungrateful, for a sense of gratitude for things given lies at the very foundation of reciprocity. Some adequate proportionality between giving and receiving love in the context of special relations is a common moral expectation, a truly universal intuition. Reciprocity is not expected in love for the stranger, which is generally unilateral, but seems to characterize friendship and other special relations.

Loving parents should have expectations regarding their children; these range from respect to emotional support and affirmation. While parental love is often unconditional and remarkably patient, reciprocation is an underlying hope. Filial love and obligation rest on an image of the family as a center of giving and re-ceiving. Just as parents are discredited when they fail to provide for their children, so children are discredited when they fail to live up to the expectation of loving parents that love be increasingly mu-tual. However much parental love requires sacrifice, it accepts love's return, even if the return of love will never be symmetrical with the more powerful parental affections. But it is, of course, parental love that initiates the flow of mutuality, and without parental love children will be less likely to take filial obligations seriously.

Philosopher Jeffrey Blustein presents the strongest case against parental expectations of filial reciprocity for love received. Blustein maintains that the duty of gratitude must be distinguished from that of indebtedness. While one can be obligated to be grateful even when what has been given was not voluntarily accepted, such is not the case when it comes to indebtedness. Young children "cannot exercise genuine choice" with respect to "being born, fed, clothed, nurtured, and educated."[24] Therefore, because "genuine choice" is not involved, presumably adult children should not feel that they owe their parents anything at all. They are not indebted because they were not at liberty.

Moreover, Blustein argues that the office of parenthood is like that of the lifeguard who, by virtue of specific social role, is oblig-ated to rescue swimmers. Lifeguards "should not demand or even expect repayment from a rescued swimmer when they were only doing their job of rescuing him." Because parents are "merely dis-charging their duties" when they care for children, they ought not to expect reciprocation. "If parents have any right to repayment from their children, it can only be for that which was either above and beyond the call of parental duty, or not required by parental duty at all."[25]

Blustein successfully undercuts manipulative expectations of par-ents who bring children into the world on the assumption that the child will be devoted to them no matter what. Yet in response to Blustein, it must be pointed out that the principle of reciprocation does not stand or fall on "genuine choice," but on the presence of parental love in the first place. True, childhood is a stage of restricted freedom, but commonly we feel a sense of debt to schools we attended and to the people who dedicated themselves to our well-being. As we grow into adulthood, there is a fairly common inclination to think that what society gave us freely in youth ought to be reciprocated. Furthermore, a good childhood is one in which "genuine choice" is frequently exercised, and increasingly so with growth into adolescence. It is not clear that the lifeguard metaphor is appropriate in this context. A parent is unlike the lifeguard, the policeman, or the fireman in many ways. Obviously, the family is a different form of community from society at large. Parents and children are bound together in a way that lifeguards and swimmers are not; the parent-child bond is simply unparalleled.

A parent may have been loving at first but less so later. Many adult children would still feel a deep loyalty to their parent in such situations, remembering acts of past parental love. Reciprocity must be placed in a much wider context than what transpires between two people at this precise moment in time. A more loyal notion of parental–filial reciprocal love would allow for filial duties beyond the point at which the parent is no longer able to love expressly, or the point where for any number of reasons that original parental love may have faded.

I have argued that filial obligation is grounded in the principle of reciprocity in love, and this is my major contention. But any affirmation of filial morality must be made realistically and with certain provisos. First and foremost, it should never be assumed that filial obligation exists without a basis in the child having experienced parental love. Secondly, it should never be assumed that filial obligation is unlimited, no matter how loving a parent has been. Such limits are discussed concretely in the next chapter.

Filial Love Inspired

I want to enrich this discussion with a narrative example of my argument that filial love is the creation and child of parental love. As proponents of narrative ethics argue, a story affects us much more than the thin experience of reciting a principle. That parental virtue is deeply causative of filial response is the focus of Dostoyevsky in one of his last novels. *The Adolescent (or A Raw Youth)* was published in 1874. The reception was unfriendly, and the book is not one of the author's best known. Yet as a study on death and growing old, it is a classic. In *The Adolescent,* Makar Evanovich Dolgoruky is a former serf, now old and gray, and the legal husband of the title character's mother. "The adolescent," Arkady Dolgoruky, relates this description by Makar of virtuous dying:

> So a pious old man must be content at all times and must die in the full light of understanding, blissfully and gracefully, satisfied with the days that have been given him to live, yearning for his last hour, and rejoicing when he is gathered like a stalk of wheat unto the sheaf when he has fulfilled his mysterious destiny.[26]

Arkady notes of Makar that "there was gaiety in his heart and that's why there was beauty in him. Gaiety was a favorite word of his and he often used it."[27] Makar seems to rejoice in the existence of things around him, whether human or nonhuman, animate or inanimate. His appreciation of the mystery of the world moves him far beyond a merely utilitarian relationship with the people and objects he encounters. He does not seek to turn the world to his advantage, and values things and people simply on the basis of their being. Arkady evidently feels this "gaiety" of heart, this mystical love for the world that is so different from mere aesthetics.

Arkady continues: "Moreover, I'm sure I'm not just imagining things if I say that at certain moments he looked at me with a strange, even uncanny love, as his hand came to rest tenderly on top of mine or as he gently patted my shoulder."[28] It is love that is Makar's chief virtue. Speaking of death he comments:

> And grass will grow over his grave in the cemetery, the white stone over him will crumble, and everyone will forget him, including his own descendants, because only very few names

remain in people's memory. So that's all right—let them forget! yes, go on, forget me, dear ones, but me, I'll go on loving you even from my grave. I can hear, dear children, your cheerful voices and I can hear your steps on the graves of your fathers; live for some time yet in the sunlight and enjoy yourselves while I pray for you and I'll come to you in your dreams. . . . Death doesn't make any difference, for there's love after death too![29]

Arkady observes that Makar likes most to talk about religion, about legends of ascetics from the remote past he had heard "from simple, illiterate folk." Makar is able to inspire love in Arkady, and gradually Arkady begins to love him.

In the love between Makar and Arkady, we are reminded of the mutual love in the traditions of Judaism and Christianity described through the covenant metaphor. The term "covenant" has been thoughtfully defined by James F. Childress: " 'Covenant' suggests a reciprocal relationship in which there is receiving and giving. But it is not reducible to a contract with a specific quid pro quo, for it also contains an element of the gratuitous which cannot be specified."[30] Participants in a covenant must be at least as other-regarding as they are self-regarding. This ethic does not require radical self-abnegation or a rejection of all reasonable self-concern. However, it does require us to transcend egocentric behavior. In regard to the ideal of an intergenerational harmony, the mutual interdependence of the covenant relationship has much to offer.

Love within covenant is fitting for the aging parent, but other-regarding love is not always encouraged among the old in our society. Rather, old age is construed as "a rainbow of promises." There is little criticism to be found of narcissistic values that diminish the integrity of some elderly persons, as Stephen Sapp has pointed out:

How much fuller might old age be if spent in some form of service to others? How much more purpose might be found for the sometimes seemingly endless time if the lost responsibilities of job and children are replaced, not exclusively with *self*-oriented recreational pastimes, but with activities that contribute to the welfare of others?

Elderly people, according to Christian thought, should be encouraged toward beneficence. Sapp claims that "older people in particular need to remember that Christ's call to serve others knows no time limit."[31]

Elderly parents within the Christian tradition might begin to think about the high dignity Jesus of Nazareth conferred on children. Elderly people, according to this vision, rather than seeking separation from the young and very young in a private world for the old—a very recent phenomenon found primarily in Western and especially American society—ought to be serving the young and one another in imitation of Christ. Somewhat paradoxically, through loving and serving the young the elderly help secure their own well-being. In a classic of modern anthropology, Leo W. Simmons examined the moral status of elderly people in primitive societies and found that they are highly regarded where they contribute most to the lives of the young: "Perhaps the simplest and most effective way of eliciting the support of others has been to render essential—if possible, indispensable—services to them." The fact is that the roles of elderly people have in the past "hardly ever been passive" at any stage in the cycle of life. Moreover, their activities have done much to influence their security. Regarding the ancient Hebrews Simmons writes: "Their security has been more often an achievement than an endowment—an achievement in which favorable opportunities have been matched with active personal accomplishments."[32]

The proposition underscored thus far is this: those elderly parents who can should, to a reasonable extent, devote energies to caring for the young (in addition to caring for other elderly persons). This is both a moral end in itself as well as a means of encouraging degrees of reciprocity from the young. Without intending to encourage any negative stereotypes of the elderly, William F. May warns against any inclination to "clutch at possessions" the "closer one gets to the final dispossession of death."[33] May emphasizes the need for virtuous behavior. He comments that in the late Middle Ages avarice was identified as the "chief besetting sin of the aged." This may mean that ageist stereotypes were common in the Middle Ages, since there is little evidence that the elderly are more prone to avarice than are other age groups—as May might have pointed out. Nevertheless, the problem of narcissism and self-centeredness pervades American society in all age groups and must be reversed insofar as this is possible.

For the adult child, commitment to an intergenerational covenant must be as firm as for the old. A genuine commitment to others is an essential beginning of covenantal relations. That I have considered the elderly first in this discussion is not meant to imply that they have missed the mark more than the adult child, although as teachers of the young they may have a special duty to set an example of virtue. Children must learn to love elderly people despite the problem of ageism. Robert N. Butler may be right to suggest that even beyond culture there is the problem of "a deep and profound prejudice against the elderly which is found to some degree in all of us."[34] Surely the elderly remind the young of mortality, of loss of beauty, vitality, memory, and the like. A fundamental fear of age is something accentuated in a culture with a passion for youth. In what has been characterized as a "death-denying society," the old are easily scorned. Ageism may, to some extent, explain any tendency of the elderly to segregate themselves from the young.

The achievement of other-regard and the demise of ageism are hindered by the eclipse of tradition that characterizes modernity. Karl Barth underlined the importance of the "teaching function" associated with the elderly, whose insights into traditions both religious and moral give them value in the eyes of the young.[35] And in relation to their own children, writes Barth, "they do not merely represent their own knowledge and experience but that conveyed to them by their own predecessors."[36] In secular modernity, the loss of tradition means that the elderly have limited opportunity to function as teachers; correlatively, the young find no valuable information in what the old convey. The loss of tradition makes it more difficult for the old to have opportunities to love the young, and thus to be viewed positively by the young. Ours is, for the most part, a revisionist's world, and a source of valued knowledge is more likely to be the latest computer software than a wise old man or woman.

Final Thoughts

In conclusion, I am driven back to theological themes. Filial love at the most profound level is a response to that most steadfastly loving parent, i.e., the Mother-Father God. In the form of love for God, filial love is perfected and issues in deep piety. All of Judeo-Christian history can be interpreted in terms of attempts at restoring the perfect love between divine parent and humanity. Religion transfers to the order of the universe the model of the human family.

In this world no human parents are perfectly loving. We need to be wary about expecting too much of parents with respect to either the depth or duration of their love. But filial love is a reciprocation upon which all genuine filial duties are based. Perhaps it is in light of inevitable parental imperfection that the Decalogue asserts the rule of filial honoring of parents, since finally the degree of unavoidable imperfection that would void filial duties is impossible to define and easily exaggerated. Since some adult children spend their lives constructing fine criticisms of their parents' actions, and since it is always easier to see the sins of others than of oneself, the categorical honor and care of parents required by the commandment may be less unreasonable than we have supposed.

Yet in the final analysis, filial love can be expected to exist only where parental love has been manifest or still remains. The law of filial piety, whether Eastern or Western, simply overlooks the requirement that parental love is the necessary condition of filial. There is nothing greater than a child's first experience of loving, since this act builds on the presence of parental love to which it is pure response. The reunion of merciful parent with prodigal child, and Jesus' use of the word *Abba,* explain to me the simple essence of being a child of God. In the ordinary bonds of love between parents and children lies extraordinary meaning, if what is eternal can be partly glimpsed in the temporal.

Familial Love:
Self-Denial
and
Self-Concern

The family is the linchpin of gender, reproducing it from one generation to the next. As we have seen, family life as typically practiced in our society is not just, either to women or to children. Moreover, it is not conducive to the rearing of citizens with a strong sense of justice. In spite of all the rhetoric about equality of the sexes, the traditional or quasi-traditional division of family labor still prevails.
    SUSAN MOLLER OKIN, *Justice, Gender, and the Family*

The choice of suicide on grounds of age has today become much more than a philosophical question. But the pragmatic context of that choice is changing as social values change. In years to come we may see an increasing acceptance of old-age suicide precisely when factors of individual rationality become intertwined with the social context: for example, the fear of becoming a "burden" on others.
    HARRY R. MOODY, *Ethics in an Aging Society*

In the previous chapters I have considered married, parental, and filial loves. This chapter draws on the earlier ones, focusing on the equal sharing of caregiving roles between men and women. Love requires loyalty and considerable self-sacrifice consistent with reasonable self-concern. If ours is a morally minimalist society in which people feel justified simply for not inflicting the wanton harm on others that has become so commonplace and banal, if ours is a time when moral idealism and beneficence have to some extent waned, then the family is perhaps too romantically conceived of as a last bastion of love. The intense solicitude that indicates the presence of love is the underlying affective impetus in familial caregiving. It is remarkable just how much family members can care for one another in times of illness, as though these are the times in which the depth of love must be tested. Indeed, the vast majority of long-term caring occurs in families at home rather than in long-term care institutions.

Some proponents of family caregiving go too far, however, in thinking that families do not require various forms of assistance in order not to exhaust their precious moral resources. One myth of American culture is that the family must be self-reliant, that it can sustain even the most onerous caregiving. But in fact wider communities are essential to sustain many, even most families in the midst of a caregiving crisis. Thus, the church has a crucial role in supporting the family not only with the narratives that give meaning to care, but with a community ready to directly assist in caring. It has been said that it takes a village to raise a child; it can be said that it takes a community to care.

Especially now that the extended family has all but vanished in the United States and is quickly disappearing in many other parts of the industrialized world, the network of caregivers that prevented too much burden from falling on any one person's shoulders is largely gone. In the nuclear family, caregiving is more exhausting because there are fewer people to share the burden. Moreover, when a caregiver within the nuclear family becomes ill or exhausted, then there is often no one to take up the slack. Thus, the extended family is in many respects preferable to the nuclear

family, which is now all we have left. But it would require huge
cultural, economic, and even architectural changes to restore the
extended family to any prominence in American culture. In the
meanwhile, many urban neighborhoods are so dangerous that families can only protect themselves rather than call for support. Daniel
Callahan is correct in asserting that a good society must step in and
support the family in various ways lest the caregiving capacities of
families be lost to exhaustion.[1]

Gender Roles

Calls for loyal caregiving in the family are further complicated by
what many women consider exploitation, for in a gendered society
direct caregiving generally falls on women when it should be shared
by men. While I accept this gender argument, it is important to
highlight that women are not all alike and that some find caregiving roles to be profoundly meaningful and inspiring. Moreover, it
is necessary to remember that caregivers can easily be dismissed as
co-opted by a culture that seems to devalue dependence based on
false myths about the virtue of self-reliance, as Gilbert Meilaender
has argued.[2] Our laissez-faire society is rooted in the Lockian myth
of an individual in a state of nature prior to society, rather than in
the Greek myths of care or the Christian narratives of love.

Susan Moller Okin refers to "equal sharing between the sexes of
family responsibilities" as the "great revolution that has not hap-
pened."[3] She makes a persuasive case for the sharing of directly caring roles by men and women, and for an end to gendered family
institutions, that is, "deeply entrenched institutionalization of sexual difference" with respect to familial and social-professional roles.
It is morally unacceptable to encourage family caregiving and self-
denial without strongly asserting that direct caregiving roles must
be as much the domain of men as of women.

The literature in Christian ethics on the proper balance between
love of self and love of other is vast. Garth L. Hallett, building
on Catholic thought, provides a precise analysis of the requirements of *agape* respecting love of self and of others through a con-

trast of six rival norms: self-preference, parity, other-preference, self-subordination, self-forgetfulness, and self-denial.[4] His main criticism of contemporary Christian ethics is that it has not developed a clear "preference-rule" to balance "mine and thine," and his criticism of the wider historical tradition is that most thought has focused on the extremes of self-preference and self-denial rather than on the nuanced distinctions betwixt and between. Hallett makes a case for self-subordination as the proper Christian norm. He is thus largely consistent with the emergent Protestant position that self-denial in the absence of the duty to love the self is an inadequate norm since it encourages manipulation and even abuse. Thus, Gene Outka and Don S. Browning, among others, affirm an other-regarding ethic that includes a significant place for love of self.[5] I fully agree with these authors that reasonable self-concern is valid in love. Yet there are times in any family when self-denial is laudatory, the cross meaningful.

The question of love and self-denial is one that I have previously examined in the context of historical theology, and I am largely in agreement with the suspicions of extreme self-sacrifice as an adequate norm for Christian ethics, although sometimes this degree of love must be freely given and should be highly valued. Certainly unselfishness and an other-regarding orientation are essential and laudable in a context of gender justice. Normatively, however, the ideal of selflessness is inconsistent with both the psychological and the social structures of human experience, and represents an exaggeration of the valid ideal of unselfishness.[6] Rather than revisit the various theological debates over self-love, I prefer here to approach the question of love and self-denial in the context of familial caregiving, since familial loves are at the center of this book. To be concrete about the burdens of caring, I shape this chapter around cases of illness that stretch caregivers to the limit.

Medical Success and Increased Need for Caregiving

So often when a parent suffers from severe dementia, a child is born with serious retardation, or a spouse becomes disabled, we directly confront situations that potentially require degrees of self-denial beyond what we anticipate or are fully prepared for. Advances in medical technology have raised new questions concerning the nature and limits of caregiving obligations within the family, for despite the myth that technology relieves us of burdens and permits greater leisure, the reality in the area of health care is quite the opposite. Persons who in a previous age would not have survived illness or disability now continue in ever-increasing dependence, and the families of people with impairment or long-term illness are frequently called upon to serve as caretakers in situations demanding considerably more self-sacrifice than was required of earlier generations. More people now live into very old age and its frailties such as progressive dementias, so that the filial love of adult children is more widely challenged if they provide direct caring. Some children have always been born with disabilities, but now we commonly attempt to save them through medical heroics and place them in the hands of parents who too frequently cannot afford this. People in the past surely had their love severely tested, but this testing is now more widespread.

Many of us know of lives that have been profoundly altered by care of elderly ill parents, children with serious impairments, or spouses with chronic illnesses both physical and mental who will never regain independence. More and more, obligations arise that family members never seriously imagined as real possibilities. The modern nuclear family, consisting of parents and children living as an isolated unit, perhaps with grandparents in the home or nearby, faces a caregiving crisis. Single-parent families as well as "blended" families of husband and wife with children from previous marriages must grapple with the question of what seriously ill family members are due and why.

Although the difficult requirements of caregiving must be acknowledged, a case can be made for an ethic of stewardship in the family—an ethic of loyal self-giving that refuses to view others as mere means to our own ends. Several criticisms apply to the work of current authors who, in light of the considerable inconvenience that stewardship can now create, appear to underestimate the creative fidelities possible within families. Additionally, public policy must recognize that caregivers themselves need to be cared for. All too often, public policy focuses only on those individuals in need after their families have found it necessary to relinquish care. Last, the technological expansion of care may well require a religiously based ethic that views caregiving as a praiseworthy and sacred vocation rather than as a hindrance to personal freedom. In this chapter these propositions and viewpoints will be developed in the contexts of conjugal, parental, and filial loves, partly as an effort to interweave the preceding chapters on these specific forms of love.

Conjugal Stewardship

Care for a chronically ill and dependent husband or wife can rarely be sustained if it relies on a love that is superficial, essentially self-interested, and lacking in steadfastness. No mere love of appraisal, with its property-based core, can easily last in the face of severe mental illness. Love requires commitment and fidelity, virtues inconsistent with egocentric motives. Gustafson rightly shows little sympathy for the "egocentric, hedonistic interpretation of the ends of marriage and family" that centers on the ethic of individual self-realization, making self-sacrifice a contradiction in terms. He prefers the image of marriage and family in which we are "stewards, deputies, or custodians of one another and of life itself." For the steward, self-denial is a moral necessity for common life, entailing a "readiness to serve others at inconvenience to one's own interests."[7] The man or woman who quests ceaselessly for wider and more varied experiences, so that all relationships become mere experiments to be abandoned in favor of new explorations, will be unable to grapple with the level of commitment that human contingency and vulnerability require.[8]

In our technological age, it has become more imperative that the solemn vows of marriage be taken seriously, as I suggested earlier. These promises encourage a spouse to achieve a form of self-fulfillment based on transcendence of self through loving another person. In commitment one purposefully accepts care for another in both the present and the future.

Some, perhaps many, fear that the technological expansion of care locks them into a life of irrevocable self-denial. When a spouse who in a previous age would have died now lives on for years in a condition of total dependence, perhaps with a form of irreversible dementia such as Alzheimer's disease, a husband or wife is confronted with tremendous challenges.[9] It may be that a purely secular perspective is inadequate to sustain fidelity in such cases; perhaps the mystery of God's own fidelity must serve as the paradigm to be mirrored in our own lives. Stewardship implies a free act of self-giving that may require a religious framework. The Jewish notion of *hesed,* or steadfast divine love in faithful covenant, and the New Testament injunction "Love one another as I have loved you" enjoin an ideal of loyal stewardship.

The direction in which the notion of conjugal stewardship points is perhaps best illustrated by the French existentialist and Catholic philosopher of love Gabriel Marcel. Marcel reacted against Jean-Paul Sartre's assumption that every human being is the enemy of the other, which interprets all human encounters as forms of conflict. For Sartre, freedom and fidelity are opposed: freedom of self demands an individualism unhampered by bonds of love and promise. Marcel prefers the ideals of mutual self-giving and faithfulness to others; he rejects self-enclosed individualism for an authentic existence of commitment to others.[10] "Creative fidelity," argues Marcel, satisfies human longings for certainty and steadfast love; it liberates persons from chaos and unpredictability. A model of conjugal fidelity, Marcel cared for his fatally ill wife over a period of years.

Yet the technological expansion of care threatens conjugal fidelity. Increasingly, to be a steward is to be penalized, for care requires ever more demanding acts of self-denial. As Robert Bellah has pointed out, within American culture many marry with such values in mind as full communication and self-expression, both of which are essentially incompatible with self-denial.[11] Such values can never sustain the moral duties toward which modern medical technology is driving us in numerous instances, i.e., greater long-term dependence on the care of others. A religiously grounded image of marriage, however, insists on stewardship as a vocation for men as much as for women, to be supported and sustained in community. Given the technological developments that have altered the biological and moral balance of earlier times, this religious framework may provide hope.

Parental Morality and Imperiled Newborns

The question of what parents owe newborns with serious impairments has recently been so thoroughly discussed that it requires little additional comment. Clearly the developments in neonatal medicine confront parents with dilemmas and pressures altogether unheard of just two decades ago. Now, huge numbers of infants with disabilities are brought home from neonatal intensive care units by parents who have almost no public entitlements to support them in the permanent duties they have sometimes willingly assumed, or perhaps have had imposed on them by an overly aggressive use of medical technology. This absence of support is particularly unjust when medical technology is used in the face of the parents' wishes to the contrary. Social workers report "chronic sorrow" on the part of many parents unable to transcend their sense of helpless despair not only because their child is not what they had hoped for, but because the economic burdens for the future are so onerous.[12] Moreover, there is strong evidence that divorce rates are high in the families of these newborns because of "burnout," loss of free time, and fatigue.[13] Helen Featherstone, herself the mother of a son with severe impairments, has written about parental response to caring in these circumstances. Normal children, she notes, exact heavy commitment, but the demands taper off as the children grow independent. Impairment can retard or even prevent this tapering process, "extending a child's dependence beyond a parent's natural strength." "A disabled child," she concludes, often "forces parents to think of their old age in ugly dismal terms."

Featherstone cites one mother's response to the burden of care as an example: "And when I project, all I see is a sleepy life of never-ending diaper changing for all of us."[14] Some parents resent the technological expansion of care and understandably long for a less aggressive form of medicine that is willing to let nature take its course.

Yet other commentators describe the ways in which families benefit from caring for a child with severe impairments. Rosalyn Darling, for instance, focuses on the stages of parental adjustment to these children. At first, she observes, parents feel helpless and depressed in the midst of what appears to be an overwhelming tragedy. With support from family and friends, however, this first stage can be quite brief. Then parents can go on to accept their child, especially if support services are available. Finally, parents enter an "advocacy stage" in which they challenge the social prejudices and difficulties that parents and families "in most cases" seem to adjust to. For the most part, in the absence of serious personal or financial difficulties, the presence of the child "seems to draw family members closer together as an ingroup facing the hostilities of the outside world."[15]

The significance of Darling's work is this: if families are given the emotional and community service support required, stewardship can be a fulfilling experience. Stewardship in the light of neonatal advances is always going to be challenging; it should not be overly idealized by those who extol the meaning and unity in acts of caring that some families discover. Nevertheless, the work of stewardship can be viewed as a creative vocation, and it is in this direction that agapic thought must press. As Gustafson comments in his argument that parents should care for a child with Down's syndrome, "Finally, my view, grounded ultimately in religious convictions as well as moral beliefs, is that to be human is to have a vocation, a calling, and the calling of each of us is 'to be for others' at least as much as 'to be for ourselves.'" Such a calling does not solve all the complex problems of family caregiving, but "it shapes a bias, gives a weight, toward the well-being of the other against inconvenience or cost to oneself."[16]

Filial Morality

As the proportion of elderly citizens in Western societies grows larger, adult children are increasingly bound by obligations to elderly ill parents. The last philosophical thinker to address himself systematically to filial morality was the British moralist Henry Sidgwick. According to Sidgwick, the obligation of children to parents is based on gratitude, that "truly universal intuition." That children have a moral duty to requite benefits is so clearly agreed upon, argues Sidgwick, that it is open to no dispute "except of the sweeping and abstract kind."[17] He allows that filial obligation might be limited in the case of a parent who has been irresponsible in fulfilling parental duties, but even in such cases he believes that adult children should serve as caretakers.

The traditionalist perspective of Sidgwick is echoed, albeit less systematically, by C. S. Lewis. Writing in 1947, Lewis concerns himself with the tendency of "moderns" to displace the moral heritage. He refers to those who claim to be cutting away "the parasitic growth of emotion, religious sanction, and inherited taboos" in order to "debunk" the merely conventional.[18] At the end of *The Abolition of Man* Lewis lists some important moral traditions that he thinks should be preserved. Under the rubric of "Duties to Parents, Elders, Ancestors," he refers to passages from most of the world religions and from many classical philosophers affirming that such duties do exist.[19] Here Lewis includes the Judeo-Christian precept "Honor thy father and thy mother." He also lists a moral dictum from the ancient Stoic philosopher Epictetus, "To care for parents."

Philosopher Jane English may too narrowly attach filial obligations to current mutual love. "What do grown children owe their parents? I will contend that the answer is 'nothing.'"[20] English grants that children may want to assist parents if a close bond of love and friendship exists, but this position places filial caregiving on the fragile basis of "spontaneous love." This raises the question of whether her definition of love as a spontaneous phenomenon is adequate, since Christian thought generally thinks of love as requiring significant degrees of loyalty, and as relatively steadfast despite times when spontaneity is absent.

I am driven back to the ordinary person who attests to commitments in the sphere of filial morality, commitments generally grounded in at least the memory of love. Everett Hall, the philosopher of "common sense realism," wrote that our knowledge of values must "find its test in the main forms of everyday thought about everyday matters in so far as these reveal commitment in some tacit way to a view or perhaps several views about how the world is made up, about its basic 'dimensions.' "[21]

The tradition of Western morality affirms filial love as an essential aspect of human experience. In addition to Hebrew Bible precepts, there is a very influential New Testament passage: "But if a widow has children or grandchildren, then they should learn as their first duty to show loyalty to the family and to repay what they owe to their parents and grandparents; for this God approves" (1 Tm. 5:4). On a more general level, 1 Timothy 5:8 reads, "But if anyone does not make provision for his relations, and especially for members of his own household, he has denied the faith and is worse than an unbeliever." This latter passage is cited by Augustine in *The City of God,* where he argues that one is to care "primarily" for those in one's own household, because "the law of nature and of society gives him readier access to them."[22] Thomas Aquinas repeats the Augustinian argument in his *Summa Theologiae* (II–II, Q. 32, art. 9). Precisely how the Christian affirmation of filial love should be interpreted is subject to considerable debate. It may well be that given the emphasis on human dignity characteristic of the early Christian movement, the elderly, like children, gained in status. Consistent with the patristic heritage, the contemporary Catholic moralist Bernard Haring maintains that one of the principal duties of children is "to assist their parents in every emergency, but especially in their old age."[23]

By and large, then, the Western heritage of ethical ideas has underscored the importance of caring for the elderly parent, despite inconvenience, so long as parents have themselves been responsible. Gratitude for parental love and respect for the aging parent as a fully dignified human being are deeply inscribed in the tradition; and it is this religious tradition that informs the strictly philosophical thinkers, however unconsciously, through Sidgwick. Between Sidgwick and the latter twentieth century, philosophers have had nothing to say about filial morality, though now the revisionism of English and others is available. Not all of the philosophers are ready to jettison the concept of loving stewardship for the aging parent. Christina Hoff Sommers, most notably, has recently written on filial morality in a manner consistent with religious tradition. Sommers warns against the consequences of the modern hostility to the moral practices and institutions "that define the traditional ties binding the members of a family or community." Before this century, she notes, "there was no question that a filial relationship defined a natural obligation."[24]

In an aging society, many adult children of elderly ill parents are faced with caregiving responsibilities of unprecedented magnitude. Feminists writing on the aging society rightly caution against having too much of the caregiving burden fall on women, who are already in a "superwoman squeeze" between job, parents, children, and spouse.[25] Certainly filial love applies to men as well as women; it is clearly unjust to place an unequal burden on women. Given the proportions of the demographic transition to an aging society, we may well be at the crossroads between stewardship and the disregard of the aged. Despite the serious pressures of technologically expanded care, the tradition of stewardship and filial love needs to be sustained. Without this tradition, moral chaos will quickly emerge. Of course for those whose parents have never been loving, and have perhaps been abusive, filial love and related obligations would not be expected to hold.

The Limits of Self-Denial

These affirmations of self-giving love should not obscure the fact that caregivers also need to be cared for. The self that is shattered by coercive abnegations of personal interests, needs, and significant desires will not be able to sustain other-regarding activities for long, if at all. All people have legitimate bodily, psychological, and spiritual self-concerns that accompany their readiness to serve others.

Each of us knows persons who, when confronted with the responsibilities of caring for a chronically ill child, spouse, or parent, have made tremendous sacrifices. Are there reasonable limits to the caregiving responsibilities in such cases? Of course there are power struggles within families that lead the elderly ill to choose a life with persons other than family members—a choice some spouses and mature children might make as well. But is there any moral justification for a family's relinquishing care of a member who desires the love and commitment that a family, at least ideally, can offer? Does stewardship require radical self-denial, or does it require balance between being for others and being for ourselves? Can a caregiver make valid appeals to integrity of self and proper self-love? Feminists have rightly pointed out that a crucial problem for women has been selflessness and self-abnegation rather than an inordinate love of self. It is not unusual for women to express the fear that the technological expansion of care will mean for them more oppressive bondage to what has commonly been termed their "experience of nothingness"—the surrendering of their individual concerns in order to serve the immediate needs of others to the extent that they do not have the opportunity to develop as independent persons.[26]

These concerns are valid. It is widely accepted that a concern for one's own well-being is a prerequisite for the self-giving that stewardship demands. Though selfless giving is often idealized, the reality is that those who care must themselves be cared for if depletion and the burnout of which the literature speaks are to be avoided. Some individuals may be able to thrive in the role of steward even if radical self-sacrifice is needed. Saints and heroes, however, are rare. Thus society must acknowledge that appeals made in the language of "obligation of self" have moral validity and that stewards can justly call for public assistance in the form of respite, counseling, and group support.

This realistic assessment of stewardship inevitably leads us to public policy. One erroneous policy position seems to ignore the needs of family caregivers: "If families would take care of the very young, the very old, the sick, the mentally ill, there would be less need for day care, hospitals, and Social Security and public resources and agencies."[27] The good family, we are told, is essentially independent and self-sufficient. It is essential that an appeal for familial caregiving not be interpreted as an alternative to necessary public support. In fact, the long-term care now required demands a policy of emotional and material support for families involved in the caregiving process. Too much public policy at present focuses on the needs of the individual whose family has relinquished care because of a lack of social and financial support. In fact, as Rosalyn Darling insists, society ought not allow families to become exhausted in the first place.

Even with an adequate public policy, however, one wonders if the challenges of home care can be met without community-wide realization of the vocation of stewardship. At present, there are few areas in the United States where the family caretaker receives his or her due. Among social service professionals a wide consensus exists that the ill and disabled are more likely to achieve their potential in family, or familylike, settings; but the family itself must not be viewed as an isolated unit. Given the frequent absence of support, we must be tolerant of those who are unable to handle the stress of stewardship and therefore must relinquish direct care. Some philosophers have argued that "ought implies can," that no person is morally obligated to do anything he or she could not have succeeded in doing however strong the motivation or his or her character. Such language does not take us too far, however, because "can" is always a matter of degree. Clearly it is tragic that family members who want to care cannot do so because of our national myth of self-reliance.[28]

The problem of caregivers left uncared for is a major one, calling for a redirection in public policy. With scarce support services, families providing home care also face the difficult problem of "competing obligations." The needs of one family member can, in conditions of scarcity, compete so seriously with those of another that the caregiver must relinquish some responsibility. Can there be a moral ordering of responsibilities? Would care for children take priority over care for the elderly because the young have had less opportunity to explore their potentials? If choices must be made, does one care first for one's children, then one's spouse, one's parents, and finally one's siblings? These questions are very difficult and even distasteful; moreover, I know of no moral theologian or philosopher who has attempted an ordering of family responsibilities. In an aging society, and in a technological culture that can prolong the lives of infants and others who not long ago would have passed away according to a more "natural" science, stewardship becomes more complicated; choices may have to be made concerning who can be cared for. I make no attempt here to develop a moral calculus or ordering of family responsibilities, and it may not be a good idea for anyone to do so. The ordering issue must nevertheless be considered by individual consciences.

Finally, caregiving in the family might be limited on the basis of "release by the promisee." As Margaret A. Farley has written, "Because the obligation to keep a commitment comes from yielding to someone a claim over me, it follows that if the claim is waived or relinquished by the recipient, my obligation ceases."[29] Adult family members might freely decide to forgo treatments that would seriously strain their families. In such a case one has not failed in one's obligation to a spouse or parent; rather, the obligation has been waived. Presumably, an individual might decide that the burden on other family members of caring for himself or herself was excessive, and therefore would choose to forgo the various technologies that have expanded stewardship.

There are valid moral reasons for limiting family caregiving responsibilities, and Farley has considered these limits with admirable insight. A proper public policy would enable persons to fulfill their roles as stewards in the spheres of filial, conjugal, and parental responsibility.

Closing Suggestions

In this chapter, I have attempted to keep the discussion of self-love and self-abnegation away from more abstract theological or philosophical considerations covered in preceding chapters. Moreover, I have wanted to press the reader to reflect on the real caregiving situations that almost everyone confronts, e.g., caring for a debilitated aging parent. It is in this mundane context that I have attempted to explore the balance between self-concern and other-regarding love.

Remarkably, while issues in family ethics have become increasingly important to many in our age of high-tech medicine, theological and philosophical ethicists have unfortunately devoted relatively little energy to this area. Yet the roles of mother or father, sister or brother, are for many the primary sphere of moral reflection and concern. Possibly the least discussed matter in the literature of moral philosophy is thus the one that most concerns people on a daily basis. The literature is equipped to deal with questions of social ethics and social justice much more than with personal ethics.

If ethics can begin to focus attention on the family as it confronts the expanded demands of love-stewardship, it can be hoped that makers of public policy will move in a similar direction. The medicalization of modern life, the technological assault on death, the difficulty many in secular culture have in accepting human finitude and mortality, and the relative absence of an ethical framework that views self-subordination positively—these aspects of modernity have burdened individual family caregivers.

Women are the ones typically called on to provide emotional support and assistance for those needing long-term care. Over the last few years, national attention has been focused on "women in the middle," on women sandwiched between job and family responsibilities. The extension of the human life span in modern societies means that "contemporary adult children provide more care and more difficult care to more parents and parents-in-law over much longer periods of time than ever has been the case before."[30]

Studies indicate that daughters or daughters-in-law are more than three times as likely as sons to assist an elderly caregiver with a disabled spouse, and outnumber men as the caregivers for severely disabled parents by a ratio of 4 to 1.[31] Although results vary somewhat from study to study, about half of these women caregivers experience stress in the form of depression, sleeplessness, anger, and emotional exhaustion.[32]

While women caregivers must be appreciated for all that they do, I am concerned that significant numbers of women are harmed by the gender expectation that they—and not men—embrace caregiving as their duty in life. Equal opportunity for women in society and the professions requires equal caregiving roles in the family.

There is a vital need to support family caregivers. Remarkably, despite the often unanticipated and unplanned-for burdens of caregiving, more than 70 percent of elderly persons with disabilities are cared for at home. The family is a crucial caring resource. At present, social policy often does little more than cheer the family on. First and foremost, society should *never* assume that caregiving obligations and capacities within the family are unlimited. There are instances of caregivers who have sacrificed themselves radically out of love for a family member and genuinely feel that they discovered themselves in the process. But more generally, extremes of self-denial ultimately take a severe toll on the caregiver, and they place the recipients of care at risk for neglect and abuse.

Society must recognize limits to caregiving for most people. Before the point of caregiver burnout is reached, it becomes the responsibility of society to provide aid. Family caregiving is a precious moral resource, and for this very reason it merits careful protection. The surest way to weaken and destroy this resource is to overwhelm it.

Precise limits will depend on individual circumstances, and will vary. But there is no need to argue about, or wait for, the precise point at which the burden of caring becomes unsustainable. Rather, we must recognize the proportions of the problem and create programs to mitigate it. If many intact families provide care that is uniquely beneficial to the recipient, then it is ethically un-sound and poor public policy to press them to the point of ex-haustion where they will in desperation surrender their parent, spouse, or child to an institution.

Love

for

Strangers

What has chaff to do with grain? says the Lord. Do not my words scorch like fire? says the Lord. Are not my words like a hammer that splinters rock?

JEREMIAH 23:29

Love your enemies and pray for your persecutors; only so can you be children of your heavenly Father, who makes the sun rise on good and bad alike, and sends the rain on the honest and the dishonest. If you love only those who love you, what reward can you expect?

MATTHEW 5:45–46

I n this chapter I leave behind the familial modes of love and consider the stranger, the alien who is outside of family or community. Love for the stranger is a moral challenge, since it lacks the encouraging expectations of reciprocity that reinforce self-giving in special relations and because we may have nothing in common with the stranger—or even find ourselves deeply repulsed. It is a love that aims at the good of an unknown person, whether psychophysical or religious, simply because that person exists. Love for the stranger welcomes response in forms ranging from an expression of gratitude to acts of reciprocal kindness. But response is not expected to the degree more typical of close ties and binding loves of participatory community, and it is certainly not required. The Good Samaritan (Lk. 10:25–37) reaches out to help the neighbor who is a stranger and thereby demonstrates a moral idealism that those unable to transcend ethnic, religious, or familial circles cannot achieve. Love for the stranger is a profound good, one that special relations must not obscure. Familial and participatory love should never exclude the stranger from moral considerability.

Love for God is in important respects demonstrated by love for the stranger who is a child of God. Jesus asked, "Who is my mother? Who are my brothers?" (Mk. 3:34) He pointed to all those around him who were doing the will of God and he refused to go outside to meet his waiting family. The moral genius of Christianity was to make the spirit of family love inclusive under the parental love of God, for "Whoever does the will of God is my brother, my sister, my mother" (Mk. 3:35). Those who do God's will become brothers and sisters in a community of faith that ultimately stands above the family in the order of loyalties. And the true strangers, those who wish to remain outside this community or who have never been introduced to it, are to be loved.

The first thesis of this chapter is that love for the stranger is essentially unconditional on the recipient abiding by any qualifications, but that when the aim of love is to draw the stranger into the community, it must be *expressed* as though it were conditional, for the community requires faith, character, and discipline. Unconditional love for the stranger can be appropriately regarded as part of the Christian ethic insofar as love intends the stranger's physical and basic psychological welfare, but a strategic conditionality is at times the appropriate norm when love intends the neighbor's religious well-being. Love in the first intention is concerned with "psycho-physical" existence, and therefore with the provision of food, shelter, health care, and the like; in the second sense, it is concerned with the "God-relation" of the neighbor.[1] Thus, one should feed and shelter a person in physical need because that person needs those things and wants them; yet one cannot be bound by the standard of expressed unconditionality when the neighbor presumably needs a relationship with God.

The religious community must make demands on those who cross the threshold, lest it be reduced to the religion of culture. Within early Christianity, there was the doctrine of the two ways, the way of light and the way of darkness, each way associated with patterns of behavior and character. The demands of the way of light separated the Christian from the way of the world.[2] In modernity, characterized by a massive flight from God and from many of the distinctive values of Christianity, the doctrine of the two ways is again deeply relevant.

Religious love, in other words, is expressed unconditionally when the intent is to provide for physical and psychological needs, on the assumption that a person is not suffering from some self-imposed regimen, e.g., a hunger strike, or would not for other competent reasons spurn such provisions. But when the goal of love is to bring the person to God, it must incorporate degrees of strategic conditionality that serve religious growth and the transformation of the beloved from "as is" to "as ought to be." By religious I mean literally *religio,* or "rebinding" to God, the classical Augustinian meaning.

A second thesis of this chapter is that love for the stranger must emerge from strong roots in the participatory community of believers who internalize the narratives, such as that of the Good Samaritan, that make love for the stranger possible. Such love can be understood in terms of a formal principle of conduct. Dewi Z. Phillips writes properly that Christian love is different from love for friends, for "I must love all men because all men are the same. They are children of God."[3] But the essential impetus for love comes from shared narratives, whether from scripture or from the stories of the saints that are part of a tradition of discourse. As Edith Wyschogrod indicates, "A postmodern ethic must look not to some opposite of ethics, but elsewhere, to life narratives, specifically those of the saints, defined in terms that overlap and overturn traditional normative stipulations and that defy the normative structure of moral theory."[4] Christians need their stories told in a community that creates love for the stranger. Thus Christian ethics, in order to enact love for the stranger, must highlight participatory love and narrative.[5]

Thesis I:
Unconditional Love and Conditional Expression

The provision of food, shelter, and medical care, as well as psychological support, should never depend on the recipient's state of soul. For centuries, Christians have served the needy in these various respects, adding to the "spirit of beneficence" in Western moral life.[6] Unconditional love views all human beings as worthy of protection from harms and of provision of goods, since they are created and valued as children of God. There is no person who lacks this basic value, for it is bestowed by the creator independent of any inherent capacities or talents. Human life is sacred because it is derived ultimately from the creativity of a loving God.[7]

The neighbor is admittedly *every* man and women, after the injunction "Love your neighbor as yourself" (Lk. 10:27). There is also love for enemies, "Love your enemies and pray for your persecutors" (Mt. 5:44). Religion at its best does break through from the field of familial love and friendship to a universal field of impersonal love. Love for all humanity as such, including the stranger, can be property-based if grounded in some universal aspect of persons, e.g., the Stoic notion of reason. It can also be interpreted as a love of bestowal, especially when human capacities dim. Beginning with the Hellenistic age, Greek antiquity developed the norm of *philanthropia,* referring to a generous hospitality even to the stranger. One Hippocratic precept is "Where there is love of humanity there is love of medical science." Influenced by the demands of Stoic ethics, the physician is to assist "even aliens who lack resources."[8] The ideal of love for humanity is found among the Stoics, Cynics, Pythagoreans, Hellenized Jews, and early Christian theologians, where *philanthropia* was often used interchangeably with *agape,* the New Testament Greek word for love of humanity.[9]

It is not clear whether the commandment in Leviticus, "Love your neighbor as yourself," originally applied to Jews only or to non-Jews as well (Lv. 19:18). However, in medieval Judaism it was applied to the non-Jew, as is clear in the writings of the rabbi-physician Moses Maimonides. In Christianity, building on Judaism, the practice of medicine was profoundly influenced by the story of the Good Samaritan, who assisted a wounded stranger by the roadside. After three centuries of persecution, Christians opened hospitals and made care of the sick an expression of love. They were unusually heroic in the leprosaria. It is argued that Christianity gave rise to a decisive change in attitude toward the sick, who now assumed even a preferential position.[10] Mother Teresa, awarded the Nobel Prize for Peace in 1979, has devoted her exemplary life to love for the homeless and sick strangers on the streets of Calcutta. It has been suggested that a postmodern moral philosophy could gain through a recovery of the saintly examples of compassion, generosity, and self-sacrifice.[11] The story of the Good Samaritan continues to spur voluntary caring in American culture.[12] The Good Samaritan and the requirement that all Christians assist the sick disinterestedly (Mt. 25:35–46) have deeply shaped Western moral culture.

Love for strangers does not fit in the field of personal ethics characterized by special relations. Partiality, special obligations, and proximity over extended periods of time roughly define the moral texture of personal ethics—we know one another, often deeply. Marriage, parental love, filial love, and friendship lie within the field of personal ethics. The second field is that of impersonal ethics, characterized by love for those whom we often do not know in the least. This field interweaves with social ethics, the concern with justice and basic social structures. Love of the remote, impartiality, and obligations to strangers lie here.

Love for strangers within Christian tradition is not based on some perceived positive attribute (property-based love) in the other but rather on value bestowed by the lover (existence-based love). By bestowal I do not mean "beauty in the eye of the be-holder"; the beloved is loved neither for an objective property nor for some bestowed property but because of the very being of the beloved. Property-based love is reason-dependent, i.e., X can pro-vide property-based reasons for loving Y. The attractive properties of the object account for the presence of love and determine its longevity.[13] Critics of a strictly property-based love believe that it leaves love too insecure, since the properties for which X loves Y may disappear, or X may no longer perceive them as attractive. They therefore introduce a love of bestowal, or a nonappraising love. While a wholly nonappraising love may be foreign to human nature, any love worthy of the word requires a security or com-mitment that goes beyond strictly appraisive categories.[14]

Love for strangers is not an acquisitive inclination seeking the agent's good, but a benevolent one seeking the other's good.[15] Ac-quisitive tendencies include desires for food, drink, possessions, and lead to merely instrumental relations with others, e.g., sexual relations without care or commitment. A strictly acquisitive love is not really love at all, because it implies indifference to the other's welfare except as a means to self-gratification, i.e., as a means of ac-quiring a good for the self, with benevolence never a controlling motive. Love for strangers is not characterized by the giving and receiving of friendship, marriage, and other forms of preferential and companionate love. Kierkegaard, in order to test the pure dis-interestedness of love's motivation, rejected these spheres of reci-procity for himself, and stated that the highest form of love is love for the dead, since surely they cannot reciprocate.[16]

The unconditional meeting of psychophysical needs is wholly profound, and one of the highest aims of love. But it is not the only aim, for any love that fits within the category of religion—the "re-binding" of the fallen person to God—is interested in more than the basic preservation of the neighbor's psychophysical welfare. It is by definition also a sacred love concerned with the values of the holy and the profane. It knows that the human being is a cup that only God can fill to the fullest. Therefore love must be concerned with more than physiological and psychological welfare. When love aims at the transforming of the recipient's inner religious life, it focuses on possibilities of perfection inherent in the other's being.

In this domain, Christian love must take on a conditional expression, although its essential form remains always unconditional. It is not that inwardly one's concern for the ultimate salvation of the neighbor is conditional, but that for the neighbor's good and for the success of love so intended, conditions are required, particularly the condition of repentance. Here *agape* is like parental love that delicately balances affirmation with rebuke, sometimes stern, intended to encourage moral and spiritual correction. Any parent will acknowledge that a wholly unconditional expression of love for children results in chaos and a failure in their moral and spiritual development. Unconditional love, when the intent is growth, creates conditions for the beloved.

A purely unconditional expression of love suggests a God who desires no reciprocity whatsoever, no movement of give-and-take with the beloved—a God for whose well-being no response would be necessary. Hence, while no Christian would doubt the high value of unconditional love in meeting psychophysical needs, it is of limited value with respect to the "God-relation" for both God and the human being. The Roman Catholic and Anglo-Catholic traditions have always recognized this, requiring acts of penance and reparation from the wayward soul. The strategic conditionality of love is captured in a passage attributed to Jesus of Nazareth and spoken to his missionary followers as they ventured forth to preach the Gospel: "Do not give dogs what is holy; do not throw your pearls to the pigs: they will only trample on them, and turn and tear you to pieces" (Mt. 7:6). No more authoritative approval of the conditional expression of love can be imagined. This is the harsh side of Jesus—the Jesus who told a young man concerned with his father's funeral to "let the dead bury the dead."

Such a statement brings to mind a critique of Anders Nygren penned by John M. Rist:

Could one have agape for anything, regardless of all value? The Christian God, of course, creates *ex nihilo*; but the Christian is faced with a given world. Within that world he lives, and as Nygren would put it, reflects God's agape. Yet he does not love indiscriminately. He does not show agape for vice. He may love the sinner but hate the sin, yet in his very doing so he is being selective. The objects of his agape are in fact considered.[17]

Presumably, the advocate of consistent unconditionality in the expression of love will respond to Rist with another passage, "I did not come to invite virtuous people, but sinners" (Mt. 9:13; Mk. 2:17). Nygren himself makes much of this passage, claiming that it turns Jewish values (*nomos* or "law") upside down.[18] Yet sinners are not exempt from discipline, obedience to divine will, and painstaking restoration, nor are the righteous disregarded by Jesus. In various passages attributed to Jesus, this is made clear: "Not everyone who calls me 'Lord, Lord' will enter the kingdom of heaven, but those who do the will of my heavenly Father" (Mt. 7:21).

This is not to suggest a new works righteousness of the Pelagian extreme; but it is to say that love requires a cooperation between God and person, with God the primary agent of love and redemption. Some degree of restitution or indemnification has perennially been thought necessary for the restoration of the God-relation. In the Genesis story, the fall of Adam and Eve could not be overlooked and casually forgiven. Instead the two were driven from Eden and a process of restoration over time began. The prodigal son had to make his way back, however painfully, from the far country to his father's house. Only when the son comes within sight of the father's house can the father run out to greet him. By turning toward home, the son demonstrated in will and action that he truly intended to return.

Nygren analyzes two New Testament parables to support his notion of unconditionality. The parables of the prodigal son (Lk. 15:11–32) and of the laborers in the vineyard (Mt. 20:1–16) both are said by Nygren to highlight the totally unmotivated character of God's love for the sinner.[19] But as Martin D'Arcy pointed out regarding Nygren's interpretation of the latter, "But here again the fact is ignored that they [the laborers] did offer themselves and that all did some labour. Their lot is quite different from those who remained outside."[20] Rist makes a similar point: "He who comes to work, even at a late hour, receives, in God's eyes, the fullest benefits of His love." Regarding the prodigal son, Nygren "concentrates on the rewards bestowed on the returning prodigal," forgetting all that the son must have painstakingly endured in order to make the journey home step by step.[21]

Nygren oversimplifies these parables by ignoring the setting of conditions. D'Arcy's contrast remains valid:

> He [Nygren] has to leave out the second half of a sentence such as that from the Book of Revelation: "they shall walk with me in white, because they are worthy." The real problem, as the great Catholic thinkers saw it, was to allow for the full force of grace and Agape and also for man's participation in the new supernatural friendship.

In essence, "The principle of give and take has to be harmonized in all phases of love."[22]

In the Beatitudes, Jesus spoke of blessing those who desire to know God, and who thereby fulfill the condition of freely willing to receive God's love: "How blest are those who know their need of God; the kingdom of Heaven is theirs" (Mt. 5:3). Those who do not know that God alone can fill the human heart fully will only revile truth. In contrast, the prepared neighbor seeks God: "Ask, and you will receive; seek, and you will find; knock, and the door will be opened" (Mt. 7:7). In this sense, love could even be interpreted as essentially conditional, although it could also still be considered unconditional in essence.

In contrast to passages that focus on the God-relation are those that deal with the other aspects of human welfare. The latter convincingly forbid any conditional expressions. The parable of the Good Samaritan teaches that all human beings should be cared for when their bodily wounds require bandages. We are never told about the spiritual state of the victim because it is irrelevant. The

117

Samaritan is not interested in bringing the unfortunate victim of robbers toward God, but seeks only to heal and preserve life. In this case, the neighbor is viewed simply as a person whose suffering elicits a compassionate response. When the aim of Christian love is specific bodily welfare, love surely does fall on the unrighteous and the righteous in accordance with need.

Considerable unnecessary theological debate over Christian love could be avoided if the different aims of love were more clearly distinguished. There is no need for an either-or approach in Christian ethics, because both the unconditional and the conditional expressions of love have their place. When the purpose of love is to heal those who suffer from ill health or some other harm, as in the case of the Good Samaritan, unconditionality must be fully expressed. However, when Christian love is manifest in its missionary intent with respect to spiritual values, when it preaches repentance and hopes to bring the recipient into communion with God as the only lasting source of true happiness, then conditionality is the apparent norm.

In the latter context, Jesus' blunt warning not to throw pearls before swine makes good sense. A Christian hospital, a Christian program to house the homeless or feed the hungry—here unconditional expression of love reigns absolutely. But with a witnessing love that seeks the God-relation for the neighbor, the limits of purely unconditional expression of love must be acknowledged.

Barth and Outka

The classical tension between unconditional love and its conditional expression can be further examined in the light of Gene Outka's interpretation of Karl Barth. Barth had the intent of missionary love in mind when he placed emphasis on the conditional expression of Christian love: "There can be no question of an extension in principle of the concept of Christian love for the neighbor into a universal love of humanity, unless we are to radically weaken and confuse it." This narrowing of the range of Christian love will, writes Barth, prove "irksome" for those who have assumed its universality without taking into account the stages of salvation history and the resistance of sinful humanity to God's word. Nevertheless, Barth maintains that this love "is still a closed circle."[23] As I interpret Barth, the question is: *Who closes the circle?* Does not the one who refuses to repent exclude him or herself?

It should not be forgotten, contends Barth, that love is related to the history of salvation—a history that is inclusive of those who live under the "sign of baptism." The neighbor to be loved "is always the fellow-man who encounters and is united with me in the context of the history of salvation."[24]

Barth can be contrasted with Nygren, who claimed that the "particularization"[25] of Christian love even within the New Testament context of the Gospel of John is a corruption of love in its original form. Rist calls it "extraordinary" that love between those who resolve to cooperate with God posed such a problem for Nygren, "for it seems natural and right that Christians should have loved one another and should have recognized the value they had each attained in their faith."[26] Paul, after all, urged the community, "Do not unite yourselves with unbelievers" (2 Cor. 6:14).

Barth emphasized that the "circle of love" is never "hermetically sealed." The community of believers hopes that its circle will continually widen, for it is open to all who meet the condition of wishing to enter. Yet consistent with this radical openness that rejects all elitism, Barth is very clear about restraints on the range of Christian love: "It may sound harsh at first, but we have to note that neither the Old Testament nor the New speaks of a love for man as such and therefore for all men; of a universal love of humanity."[27] Barth accepts universal love on the level of physiological and psychological need, so that to a degree he may overstate his suspicion of universality. But he also makes room for the conditional expression of love.

Those who question this interpretation of Barth are directed to Gene Outka's thoughtful work. Outka finds conditional expression of love to be quite central to Barth's ethics and is critical of this. Outka's position, posed as a counter to Barth, is that a "definite faith state" ought not to condition whether and how the agent loves. Outka is partly correct: perhaps the faith state should not condition *whether* we love, but it certainly ought to condition *how* we love. Outka rejects "the faith-love correlation" that "places agape in the community as that circle where meaningful communication is possible." He argues that the "bulk of the literature" he has examined indicates that love is "universal in its range." His main reference here is to Nygren: "Nygren, for instance, accepts that agape plainly includes this feature."[28]

But as indicated earlier, the prodigal son met a condition for receiving the father's love, namely, he had a change of heart and actively turned to his father for forgiveness. And in the parable of the laborers (Mt. 20:1–16), God rewards even those who have worked only an hour because they have at least met some minimal condition that indicates their sincere commitment to God's kingdom. Divine love in its witnessing intent may be extraordinarily generous, but this generosity is directed toward those who manifest the willingness to respond. Otherwise, the beatitude "Blessed are those who do hunger and thirst after righteousness, for they shall be filled" would be reduced to the nonsensical, and "Blessed are the pure in heart, for they shall see God" would be inexplicable. Barth, when playing the part of the spiritual evangelist, is appropriately skeptical of unconditionality.

Outka persuasively articulates that domain in which unconditional love should be manifest in its full expression. He can then apply his theory of agape to justice in health care, for example. The "welfare" of all persons—"understood in both a physiological sense (e.g., for food, drink, shelter, and health) and a psychological one (e.g., for continuous human affection and support)"—should be the concern of agape, he writes.[29] Barth surely concurs that no person suffering from hunger or pain must meet moral or spiritual conditions. But this verity need not obscure the necessity for a more conditional expression of love that is relevant when the God-relation is intended.

Jack T. Sanders writes that in the Gospel of Matthew, sharp distinctions are made between "Christians and non-Christians" (Mt. 7:21). Only those who do the will of the Father will enter into the kingdom of heaven (Mt. 7:21). Christian love, contends Sanders, "involves only the carrying of the Gospel to the world, not unlimited care exercised toward one's fellow man."[30] In the Gospel of Matthew, he argues, insider–outsider distinctions are more sharply drawn than in the Gospel of Luke with its parable of the Good Samaritan, but they are no sharper than the distinctions drawn in the Johannine writings, or in the community-centered epistles of Paul. The distinction in ethics that Sanders detects between gospels is consistent with my thesis that the purely unconditional expression of love is appropriate in one context but not the other.

Bringing the gospel to the world is *to the world,* not merely to the communuity of faith. The insider–outsider distinction only arises when and if those outside the community impertinently reject the gospel. The intent of Christian love in Matthew is for the most part religious conversion. Insider–outsider distinctions are inevitable in such a context. But in Luke, the intent is more often to preserve the neighbor from bodily harms. Luke was himself a physician, concerned with benefiting those suffering from illness. The Beatitudes in Luke refer to the literally poor, rather than to Matthew's "poor in spirit," and those without basic material goods are made the responsibility of the Christian regardless of their being outsiders. Luke, then, stresses unconditional love aimed at protecting all persons from harms, while Matthew stresses spiritual witness. Thus, these gospels both make a necessary contribution to the full purposes of love, one emphasizing its conditional and the other its unconditional manifestations.

The Condition of Deep Longing

What, more precisely, is the essential condition that love requires when it intends the God-relation? The Anglican ethicist Helen Oppenheimer suggests this:

It would be no small thing if we could get back to the deep longing for the love of God that has made the great saints. "If

you long for the Sabbath," St. Augustine told his congrega-
tion, "you are not ceasing to pray . . . You will lapse into si-
lence if you lose your longing." We may well wonder if that
is what is really wrong with the church today.[31]

It is the striving love for God, which surfaces as part of our human
ontological structure. Oppenheimer's proposition that "the deep
longing for the love of God . . . has made the great saints" is significant. "Our capacity to want," she writes, "is part of His image
in us." Moreover, "The wanting, striving character of our love is
part of our created goodness, not just part of our sinfulness. Christian redemption is restoration to our proper kind of wanting, not
the quenching of want."[32] Of course God descends to human beings in accordance with grace, "yet this cannot mean that God descends to man's moral and religious level, for who would accuse
God of becoming a sinner in order to obtain fellowship with
man," contends Rist.[33]

At a minimum, the condition for love must be repentance and
longing, as in the case of the prodigal. This longing is everything
Nygren described it as—acquisitive, upward, requiring of human
effort, egocentric (sublimely so), based on want or need, deter-
mined by the goodness of its object and its value. Longing is good
not just because it derives from the ontological structure given to
human beings by a loving creator, as Augustine insisted, but also
because it sets a condition of atonement that allows for the reunion
of the estranged. The wayward must atone. As Richard Swinburne
argues regarding general human relations,

> A wrongdoer is under an obligation to deal with his guilt,
> subjective and objective; and the "dealing with" the guilt is
> not unnaturally seen as removing it. In so far as guilt is analo-
> gous to a debt, it can be removed either by the action of the
> wrongdoer (in some way) paying it off; or by the action of the
> victim (in some way) taking compensation.[34]

Atonement, contends Swinburne, includes repentance, apology,
reparation, and penance. "I remain guilty for hurting you," he

writes, "if I do not do what I can to remove the harm I have done you." Of course, the final act belongs to the victim—God in this case—to forgive. But forgiveness should not come too easily; it should certainly not come unconditionally. According to Swinburne, "It is both bad and ineffective for a victim of at any rate a serious hurt to disown the hurt when no atonement at all has been made." The wrongdoer needs to take seriously the harm that was done, lest the harm be repeated. Humans need to take with utmost seriousness actions with injurious consequences for God's affective center. As Swinburne notes, "The man who seeks to do the best will make atonement and use the atonement made available to him by others to purge himself from past wrongdoing."[35]

Repentance and deep longing for God are acts of atonement that set conditions upon which the restoration of communion between God and self can occur in a reliable manner. Thus can God entrust her/himself to us. This last claim requires considerable theological elaboration, only some of which I offer here.

Conditionally Expressed Love and Divine Pathos

The image of a suffering God has won considerable support in twentieth-century Jewish and Christian theology.[36] No fully systematic argument for divine suffering need be mounted here; for my aim is limited to pointing out the implications of the hypothesis of such suffering for theories of Christian love. An aspect of a theology of divine suffering is that God has an affective center, inclusive of the range of emotions from joy to grief. A recognition of this center is thoughtfully articulated by a great number of revisionist theists, some of them in the tradition of process theology, others in the dialogical tradition of Buber.[37]

Oppenheimer suggests that we should compare rather than contrast God's love with human love. "When we have emphasized for all we are worth the divine faithfulness of agape," she writes, "surely we can then enrich our idea of what Christian love properly is by adding, not subtracting, the warmth of eros and the appreciativeness of philia." To God Oppenheimer ascribes both a love that bestows value on the unworthy and a love that rejoices in the value that its object achieves. She cites the mystic Julian of Norwich to press her argument: "But he wants us quickly to attend him, for he stands all alone, and he waits for us continually, moaning and mourning until we come. And he hastens to bring us to him, for we are his joy and delight, and he is the remedy of our life."[38] Human longing, concludes Oppenheimer, is after the image of God, who longs as well.

Love for God is the most essential human purpose not just for the sake of human happiness but for divine as well. This view is of course contrary to the ontological scheme in which God cannot truly need human response lest a higher order of being find fulfillment in a lower. When Martin Buber asks, "But do you not know that God needs you—in the fullness of His eternity needs you?" he captures the need-love underlying the divine hope for the restoration of human responsiveness.[39] The Hebrew Bible refers to the divine joy that issues from human responsiveness. It is replete with analogies to relations between father and child, lover and beloved, bridegroom and bride. The possibility of joy is accompanied by the possibility of pain. Few passages illustrate this better than Hosea 11:1–4:

> When Israel was a boy, I loved him; I called my son out of Egypt; but the more I called, the further they went from me; they must needs sacrifice to the Baalim and burn offerings before carved images. It was I who taught Ephraim to walk, I who had taken them in my arms; but they did not know that I harnessed them in leading-strings and led them with the bonds of love—that I had lifted them like a little child to my cheek, that I had bent down to feed them.

The divine suffering that issues from love unreciprocated is also evident from Isaiah 1:2–3:

> Hark you heavens, and earth give ear, for the Lord has spoken: I have sons whom I reared and brought up, but they have rebelled against me. The ox knows its own owner, and

the ass its master's stall, but Israel, my own people, has no knowledge, no discernment.

Passages such as these have led many modern theologians to view God as suffering.

Only a divine love with corrective conditions meant to discourage human waywardness can provide a lasting solution to the problem of divine *pathos.* If God suffers from love unrequited, then the squandering of God's love is a serious matter. Were all God's needs for reciprocity fulfilled internally, then the unconditional expression of love in this context would make theological sense. But if God's needs can only be completely fulfilled in relation with human beings, then reciprocity is theologically necessary. Of course the very suffering of God is the indication of a divine solicitude that ensures the essential unconditionality of love.

Thesis II:
Participatory Love and the Stranger

I view it as serendipitous that in the New Testament, the two most frequently used words for love are *agape* (universal and nonselective) and *philia* (particular and selective). In the Johannine writings, both these words are interspersed. On the whole, the Johannine writings emphasize love for friends in faith, while the synoptic Gospels place more emphasis on love for enemies and strangers.[40] Having both forms of love is important, because *agape* cuts into friendship and elevates it from the ambiguities of self-centeredness while *philia* cuts into *agape,* to empower or ground it in a community of faith and narrative. Paul J. Wadell describes the importance of the participatory community:

> The moral life is the seeking of and growing in the good in the company of friends who also want to be good. Friendship is the crucible of the moral life, the relationship in which we come to embody the good by sharing it with friends who also delight in the good.[41]

Growth in virtue requires friendships in faith with people who are at one with us in desiring to be good. Friendships, he continues, "come to be through goals that are shared, through common interests and concerns, but those very goals that entice us come to be only through the friendships they create."[42] Wadell understands that many theories of *agape* have placed friendship on the fringe "because friendship is preferential love."[43] Preferential and special relations are often viewed as detrimental to universal, selective love. However, I believe that they are the *sine qua non* of love for the stranger. Wadell puts this point eloquently:

> What friendship sets out to achieve is one thing if the friends aim to secure excellence in Athens, another thing if they aim for the Kingdom of God. Part of the reason philia is so often overruled by agape is that it is interpreted *apart from the narrative that allows it to be integral to the Christian life.* . . . Friendship both born from and seeking the Kingdom may be exactly the kind of love which enables us ultimately to be friends of the world. In that case, we do not leave preferential love behind, we extend its domain.[44]

The tension is not between friendship and universal love, but between friendship that seeks the ultimately all-inclusive kingdom of God and friendship that does not. *Agape* is not fully distinct from friendship. It merely "describes the ever-widening scope of a friendship whose members are trying to be like God. With *agape* we come, like God, to make friends with the world."[45] Christian friendship expands at the intersection of the church and the world, where there are tensions that cannot be quickly dissolved.

A Concluding Refrain

Perhaps the most valuable aspect of the Christian tradition has been love for the stranger. Such love provides for the just and the unjust in the domain of psychophysical needs, and our culture needs more of it. Yet there are other needs. I have argued that with regard to love in its missionary intent, a strategically conditional love is sometimes appropriate for the well-being of both God and creature.

Unconditional love need not be opposed to practical wisdom. This virtue is necessary especially when it comes to applying love to the external order. Thus, even if love is viewed as unconditional in all of its aims, the proper mode of external treatment will vary from case to case. This is all I am arguing here.

Finally, while I have brought into question the thesis that Christian love is unconditional in its expression with regard to the God-relation, I nevertheless acknowledge that unconditional expression has value as well. First, the unconditional expression of love protects against self-righteous judgmental attitudes that view all those outside the circle of faith as unworthy of spiritual concern. Faith is a mysterious phenomenon, and not all those outside the circle of faith are without it. True, "He who is not with me is against me," but it is not always clear "who is with me." Moreover, it is imperative to avoid what H. Richard Niebuhr termed henotheism, or the worship of a closed circle. Second, from a noble motive, fraternal correction based on the meeting of conditions can go on to manipulation. Finally, love in its missionary aim should always be open to the enlarging of the circle of faith, and the ideal of unconditionality does encourage outreach.

Strategic conditionality in love for the stranger with regard to sacred values is essential for the discipline of a community of friends in faith. Without some conditions, e.g., accepting a central creed, finding meaning in essential rituals, or adhering to basic spiritual and ethical standards, the community lacks all distinction and becomes little more than the religion in the image of its surrounding culture. So the stranger can be loved unconditionally through the provision of basic psychophysical needs, but the community of participatory love exists within the context of salvation history and must therefore maintain its identity against the acids of a world that is often hostile. Discipline and *nomos* are necessary for continued survival in any meaningful sense, and it is through this discipline that the communitarian base from which love for the stranger emerges can survive. Love for the stranger, as a matter of intentionality, can always be unconditional insofar as the believer hopes for the transformation of the stranger into the way of faith. But in practice conditions must be imposed for the stranger's sake, as in the classic doctrine of the two ways, and for the sake of the viability of an always imperiled community of faith entrusted with preserving for future generations the memory of God's love. It is arguable that liberal Christianity has faded in American culture in large part because it applied the ideal of unconditional love too widely and set aside the more intense religious and moral demands that make Christianity an alternative to the wider culture. Meanwhile, more conserving (demanding) churches have prospered.

An Order of Love:
Close Ties
and
Strangers

Humanity is loved in general in order to avoid having to love anybody in particular.

CAMUS, The Rebel

Hardly any moral philosopher, these days, would deny that we are each entitled to favor our loved ones. Some would say, even more strongly, that we ought to favor them, that this is not simply a moral option. This notion of partiality toward loved ones is lately gaining wide philosophical acclaim. (Ordinary people, fortunately, have held this view for quite some time.)

MARILYN FRIEDMAN,
"The Practice of Partiality," Ethics, vol. 101.

In the previous chapter, love for the stranger was strongly affirmed. But what is the proper moral balance between love for the stranger and love for those who are near and dear? This is one of the great questions in the history of moral thought both Eastern and Western. It was addressed by both Augustine and

Thomas Aquinas under the rubric of *ordo caritatis,* and has been re-stated recently by the Catholic ethicist Louis Janssens: "But at every moment our particular action can only benefit some, e.g., ourselves, a neighbor, a certain group. Why do we act for the well-being of this person or this group rather than for the advantage of others (the classical problem of the *ordo caritatis*)?"[1] Stephen J. Pope has criticized even the Catholic tradition, which was perennially sophisticated in responding to this question, for recent neglect of the *ordo caritatis.*[2] I suspect this neglect is related to the fact that so much contemporary Catholic ethics focuses on issues of social justice and liberation that the earlier attention to the familial sphere has appeared of little significance. But it is difficult to separate issues of distributive justice from issues of familial love and parental responsibility.

There are people who do good for near and dear ones too exclusively, giving insufficient attention to strangers. They make an idol of their closed social system and express no solicitude for those outside of it; they deny the universal loyalty grounded in the Christian assumption that no one is outside God's solicitude. This is why the family *needs* the community of faith that is open and dedicated to all people, the Beloved Community of which Josiah Royce wrote that saves us from limited loyalties and enmity.[3] Western monotheism is radical in requiring religious and moral suspicion of narrow loyalties. This too partly explains why contemporary liberal Christianity has emphasized cross-national concerns of peace, justice, and rights, leaving aside in-depth discussion of the family.

Yet however valid, such suspicions of the family must not hide the equally significant reverse problem, that of loving strangers while ignoring near and dear ones. The stranger should not be loved *instead* of friends and family, but in addition to them. Moreover, it is difficult to love strangers in any substantive sense until one learns what love is in the crucible of the family. How is love for family and friends properly balanced with love for humanity in general? Furthermore, should we be suspicious of claims of love for humanity by people who are failing in special relations?

The following section responds to this last question through a brief exposition of writings by Albert Camus, Charles Dickens, and William Holmes McGuffey. The rest of this chapter is an attempt to reformulate the idea of an order of love, only in the most general and flexible terms, because surely there must be considerable heterogeneity between individuals.

A Literary Introduction

When Albert Camus describes the condition of modern moral consciousness in his *The Fall,* he does so through the confessions of Clamence, an expatriate Frenchman in a seedy Amsterdam bar. Clamence recalls his past life as a highly respected lawyer and champion of noble causes. On the streets, Clamence helped the blind along crosswalks, lent a hand "pushing a stranded car," and bought papers from the Salvation Army.[4] This sounds impressive, but then Clamence confesses. Regarding personal relations, he is a libertine who manipulated woman after woman, admitting that "I never loved any of them." He laments that genuine love entirely avoided him, and that he has a "congenital inability to see in love anything but the physical." As for friends, Clamence had none: "To make up for this, their number has increased; they are the whole human race."[5] Having failed in friendships and all other special relations, he found love of humanity the easier alternative. But such love was only a thin veneer over the "selfishness wound up in my generosities." Renowned for his generosity, Clamence confesses "how much a part of my soul loathed" invalids and the "lousy proletarian."[6] Yet he much enjoyed the social recognition that his reputation for beneficence ensured.

The Fall teaches, among other things, that it is easy to "love" people who are fleeting presences because we do not have to remain with them long enough to be offended by their inevitable human imperfections. For Clamence, to toss a coin in the poor box or to speak eloquently of all humanity does not require that any particular person be continuously present. It is hard to steadfastly love the near and dear ones whom we see and know, for we become aware of their faults. Hence the French adage, "I love humanity, it is only people I detest."

Charles Dickens approached this form of moral failure through the character of Mrs. Jellyby in his novel *Bleak House*. Dickens, for all his concerns with the suffering of the working class during England's industrial revolution, was a harsh critic of people who take up social causes to the neglect of their children and immediate neighbors. Mrs. Jellyby has "a curious habit of seeming to look a long way off," as though she could see "nothing nearer than Africa." She would utter "beautiful sentiments" about "the Brotherhood of Humanity," but was neither emotionally present for her children nor particularly interested in them. Likewise, she neglects her neighbors. Mrs. Jellyby "swept the horizon with a telescope in search of others," while failing in "her own natural duties and obligations."[7] Her daughters were deeply harmed by her inattentiveness.

An especially astute discussion of this moral disengagement from special relations and from community is found in a dialogue entitled "True and False Philanthropy" by William H. McGuffey, an American educator and preacher whose *Newly Revised Eclectic Reader* was perhaps the single most influential book for American students in the mid-nineteenth century. Mr. Fantom begins: "I despise a narrow field. O for the reign of universal benevolence! I want to make all mankind good and happy." Mr. Goodman responds: "Dear me! Sure that must be a wholesale sort of a job: had you not better try your hand at a *town* or *neighborhood* first?" Mr. Fantom is identified as a philosopher too full of theories to "do a little paltry good to his next neighbor." "I wish," he exclaims, "to see the whole world enlightened." Mr. Goodman suggests that "one must begin to love somewhere; and I think it is as natural to love one's own family, and to do good in one's own neighborhood, as to anybody else." He continues, "And if every man in every family, village, and country did the same," all these loves "would fit with a sort of dovetail exactness," and all people would be cared for. But Mr. Fantom has a reply: "Sir, a man of large views will be on the watch for great occasions to prove his benevolence." So, concludes Mr. Goodman, all Mr. Fantom's opportunities for "a thousand little, snug, kind, good actions slip through his fingers in the meanwhile." Goodman laments of Fantom, "And so, between the great thing that he *cannot* do, and the little one that he *will not* do, life passes, and *nothing* will be done."[8] This little American dialogue speaks powerfully—no one can love humanity in general until they learn to love first the one and then the other particular persons right in front of them.

Moral Tradition and Partiality

Mr. Goodman's sentiments are rooted in perennial morality. Augustine acknowledged that all people are to be loved, "but since you cannot be good to all, you are to pay special attention to those who, by the accidents of time, or place, or circumstance, are brought into closer connection with you."[9] As though by "a sort of lot," wrote Augustine, some people happen to be nearer to the moral agent than others. Augustine's point is that as embodied and temporal creatures, human beings are simply unable to love all humanity, except in intention. His emphasis on beneficence to those in closer connection to the moral agent by virtue of mere accidents of time and circumstance is a striking contrast to the modern liberal philosophical assumption that we only have duties of beneficence in relations that are freely entered into rather than simply given, such as child to parent. In this, Augustine followed the Stoics, as did Aquinas, who provides an account of the order of love in question 26 of his *Summa Theologiae (secunda secundae)*, consisting of no less than 13 articles. Aquinas argues that we should love those who are connected by "natural origin" most, except when they are "an obstacle between us and God." We might well differ from his conclusion that we should love our parents more than our children, and our fathers more than our mothers because men provide the "active principle" in conception (II–II, q. 26, a. 10). Nevertheless, Aquinas takes seriously the notion that due to human finitude we cannot actively love everyone equally, and therefore an ordering of love is essential to the moral life.

The idea of an ordering of beneficence, like every legitimate principle, can be grossly misused if associated with a patriarchy or some other troublesome set of social assumptions. Nevertheless, as Sidgwick noted, we should not resolve "all virtue into universal and impartial Benevolence," as though from the viewpoint of the moral agent the well-being of any one person is "equally important with the equal happiness of any other, as an element of the total."[10] Ethical theory ought never to swing too far from thinkers like Thomas Aquinas, Bishop Butler, Adam Ferguson, Adam Smith, and Sidgwick, who believed firmly in "the Order in which Individuals are recommended by Nature to our care and attention."[11] It is reasonable to do more first for those closest to us for whom we are particularly responsible. Smith says that it is a mistake to be like "Marcus Antoninus; that while he employed himself in philosophical speculations, and contemplated the prosperity of the universe, he neglected the Roman empire."[12]

There is no need to apologize for certain people with whom one has been born into proximity, or with whom one freely chooses and develops proximity over time. Our moral lives are timeful rather than timeless. Strict impartiality theories seem to ignore this fact, and threaten to dilute the beneficial role of highly personal altruism rooted in a history of ongoing relationships. To some extent, we must leave the greatest happiness of the greatest number to God. As Smith suggested, "The care of the universal happiness of all rational and sensible beings, is the business of God and not of man."[13] I believe that each individual contributes much to love of humanity in general by providing personal and deep love to those near and dear, since the cumulative effect of all such contributions is that everyone is deeply loved as we all do our small part well and intensely.

There have always been and will always be comparatively permanent relationships, including kinship and friendship. The impartial spectator, the ideal observer, the original position, and so forth are all brothers (or sisters) under the skin. They all require a fictional leap beyond human experience and moral agency as most people know it. It is as though ethical theory somehow became

Gnostic, taking the body and biological nature, as well as the limitations of time and space, as prisons from which to escape into the world of pure spirit. Impartiality run wild delegitimizes legitimate proximities. Nothing has moral value, it might be asserted, unless it takes "the view from nowhere." Yet this devalues the moral sphere in which most human beings spend most of their time and in which they meet with most of their quandaries, i.e., family and friendship. The Enlightenment is Gnostic insofar as it seems to have stripped the self of its self by suggesting that special relations are troublesome obstacles to universal duties. A more human ethics pays attention to both the pull of special relations and the call of humanity as a whole.

No final ethical formulation details exactly what the balance between these domains of love should be. I cannot say exactly how much the physician should sacrifice the well-being of spouse and children in order to serve in an overcrowded clinic day after day to the midnight hour. It would be overly rigid to lay out a specific order of beneficence, e.g., to always assist sibling before friend, child before spouse, or parent before nearby neighbor. There is inevitable variation in the particular loves and correlative commitments that individuals develop within the sphere of proximity. However, as a general point, this sphere has some degree of priority over that of strangers.

Fortunately, ethical theory over the last decade has started to take up the order of beneficence, although recast as the partiality/impartiality debate. Impartialists have, as Marilyn Friedman describes, clustered ethical theory around some "fictional images," such as Rodrick Firth's "ideal observer," which she characterizes as omnipercipient, omniscient, dispassionate, uncreaturely, but "otherwise normal." Of course, the position of the impartial spectator or the ideal observer is useful in some ethical areas, such as in a court of law, or in certain redistributions. "But this is hardly a way to treat loved ones," writes Friedman.[14] However valid impartiality is, it is not the whole of ethics. Lawrence C. Becker points out that while morality "requires (at least sometimes) that we not play favorites, or manipulate rules to our personal advantage, or make ad hoc exceptions for ourselves," there are other times when impartiality is inappropriate:

> What makes this problematic is the evident foolishness of following this logic to its apparent conclusion—that is, to the conclusion that we must act with perfect Godwinian impartiality in every aspect of our lives and with perfect Kantian attention to universalizable principles.[15]

Human beings are finite creatures, for whom universal beneficence is impossible in practice, if not in intent. The embodiedness of human experience within space and time makes this so.

From proximate relations arise proximate loves. This mainstay of traditional morality, the ordering of love, is difficult to explain within the framework of the highly individualistic Enlightenment philosophies of the self. Yet our duties of beneficence are equal only in a most abstract way; in real life, duties are often laid down in a hierarchy and are to be fulfilled proportionately. It is not the case that familial relations are no more binding on moral agents than the claims of strangers. Such a view is counterintuitive, or inconsistent with moral experience as most people know it. To save one's own child rather than someone else's, were the choice necessary, is something for which no parent should be criticized. Our relations to and duties toward near ones are part of our substance as human beings living within biologically given relational structures. These relations define partially at least, and sometimes wholly, our obligations and duties. This ordered love holds, even if we resolutely affirm the idea of love for humanity. Thus, we hold it tragic when any individual achieves much professionally to benefit humanity but fails miserably in the sphere of family love.

To ignore proximity and timefulness is to ignore most of the everyday moral dilemmas that weigh heavily on the conscience of most people. The Anglican moralist Joseph Butler, in his discussion of love of neighbor, emphasized the importance of removing "prejudices against public spirit." Butler was as suspicious of "private self-interest" as any impartialist. Yet following both Stoic and Christian precedent (*philanthropia* and *agape*), he does not consider beneficence a "blind propension," but one "directed by reason." He continues that "the care of some persons, suppose children and families, is particularly committed to our charge by nature and Providence; as also that there are other circumstances, such as friendship or former obligations, which require that we do good to some, preferably to others."[16]

Justice and Special Relations

Most of us would allow that with respect to acts of beneficence and moral idealism, special attention to family, friends, and immediate community makes moral sense. But a dilemma arises when the benefits we provide for those near and dear go far beyond essential needs while strangers suffer from injustice insofar as their minimal human needs are ignored. In other words, a problem of injustice arises when special relations sap our resources and energies at the cost of huge distributional inequalities between the haves and the have nots. For this reason, justice requires degrees of redistribution based on a solicitude for those people who are in harm's way. Justice is the fruit of love for the stranger and demands a considerable degree of impartiality. (Obviously, in some areas such as criminal justice this impartiality must be absolute.)

But the justice of redistribution becomes unjust when it forces parents to support some morally legitimate cause to the extent that the burdens of that payment would make it impossible for them to care adequately for their own children. Modern theories of distributive justice, like theories of beneficence, tend to ignore the family as a mediating structure between the individual and society. Predicated on an atomistic view of the self, they bury the social fact that between the individual and society are morally meaningful proximate relationships.

It is remarkable that this dimension of human social experience is so little discussed in contemporary philosophical writings. This may be because family loyalties have been interpreted by some as detracting from the public good. As Lawrence C. Becker writes, "Philosophers have long been divided about whether or not familial relationships are subversive of other social structures, especially those in the 'public' sphere." The priority sometimes afforded family relations has been associated with the perpetuation of "unjust property arrangements, and deeply entrenched, self-perpetuating inequality of opportunity."[17] Plato, in his *Republic,* argued for the elimination of family relations altogether among the Guardians, and in his later dialogue the *Laws* he still advocated severe regulation of the family. Even in these cases Plato is talking about an ideal *polis* that never was. Aristotle, in the first two books of his *Politics,* retrieved family life as a good, and the Romans followed suit. Cicero referred to the family as the "seedbed of the state."[18]

Following Aristotle, Cicero, and Thomas Aquinas,[19] one philosophical school takes seriously the social value of family relations and obligations. Their philosophy of the self takes into account biologically based roles and relations, and views the uniquely powerful duties that correlate with these roles as socially beneficial. Often, families provide a uniquely loving environment for their members, and can provide economic support that would otherwise come from the state. This is a social and individual good.

Now surely family relations and feelings can detract from social and distributive justice when they become ideologically absolutist, and thereby diminish tolerance for that necessary redistribution of wealth that provides basic goods for those persons who clearly are unable to care for themselves. On the other hand, those who, like Plato or Marx, would dismantle the family in order to ensure the common good have always discovered that the family has bounced back as spiritual enthusiasm fades. Utopian efforts to ignore and even destroy the family inevitably result in dystopian tyranny. As Josiah Royce wrote, "But after all, fidelity and family devotion are amongst the most precious opportunities and instances of loyalty."[20]

No theory of justice that fails to strike a reasoned balance between the family and the common good or total utility is adequate; moreover, in most cases respect for familial loyalties contributes to the common good. A theory of justice requires a principle of *subsidiarity,* the notion, characteristic of Catholic social thought, that it is a disturbance of right social order to assign to a greater and higher association (the state) what a lesser and subordinate organization (the family) can do, or to seriously compromise the economic autonomy of the family through excessive redistribution.

But many modern theories of justice have lost touch with subsidiarity. They want to begin the theory of justice at some fictional zero point, rather than build on and harness the realities of familial ties. In the most respected modern philosophical theory of justice, John Rawls places his hypothetical decision makers in the "original position," and allows that "each person in the original position should care about the well-being of some of those in the next generation."[21] But this passage is the only one that comes remotely close to a concern with the family on the part of those behind the "veil of ignorance." Only toward the end of this massive work do we discover what bias prevents the author from a thicker view of the self: "Of course, in a broader inquiry the institution of the family might be questioned, and other arrangements might indeed prove preferable."[22]

It is a credit to the libertarians that, despite their unconscionable individualism, they account for the social nature of the self with respect to family relations. Hayek, for instance, argues that justice must make good use of "the natural partiality of parents for their children." Moreover, "once we agree that it is desirable to harness the natural instincts of parents to equip the new generation as well as they can, there seems no sensible ground for limiting this to non-material benefits."[23] Robert Nozick, who like Hayek rejects all "patterned" theories of distribution, observes that nonlibertarians have great difficulty acknowledging the social importance of families: "To such views, families are disturbing; for within a family occur transfers that upset the favored distributional pattern."[24]

It is unfortunate that a theory of justice such as that of Rawls, which is on the whole more adequate than that of the libertarians since it takes reasonable equality of condition seriously, is ambivalent toward the family and ultimately disregards it. Rather than hand the domain of family relations over to the libertarians, I suggest that the better alternative to Rawls on this matter is Michael

Walzer, whose method is more inductive and concerned with psychological realities.

Walzer begins with empirical particularities of distinctive spheres of justice, of which the domestic sphere is one. He notes that Plato set out to abolish "special affections," and the family in particular, for the purpose of the common good. However, Walzer rejects Plato and the wider historical tradition of antifamilialism that Plato set in motion. I quote Walzer's impressive passage in full:

> For it is a loss, and one that is likely to be resisted by most men and women. What we might think of as the highest form of communal life—universal brotherhood and sisterhood—is probably incompatible with any process of popular decision making. The case is the same in moral philosophy. A number of writers have argued that the highest form of ethical life is one where the "rule of prescriptive altruism" applies universally and there are no special obligations to kinfolk (or friends). Faced with a choice between saving my own child or someone else's from an imminent and terrible danger, I would adopt a random decision procedure. It would be much easier, obviously, if I were not able to recognize my own children, or if I had no children of my own. But this highest form of ethical life is available only to a few strong-minded philosophers or to monks, hermits, and platonic guardians. The rest of us must settle for something less, which we are likely to think of as something better: we draw the best line that we can between the family and the community and live with the unequal intensities of love.[25]

Walzer reminds us that however much the philosophers and hermits choose to ignore the moral importance of familial affections and obligations as they develop an ethic for strangers alone, most of us reject such reductive views of our duties. Moreover, even if universal brotherhood and sisterhood is taken as the highest norm, it is inapplicable insofar as most of us would not be willing to abide by it. However much deductive theorists spin out theories of strict impartiality with regard to duties, Walzer points out that human beings do establish priorities that take the family into account.

Theories of justice might take the Scottish Enlightenment as a starting point, for it stressed the moral value of family affections, and of the affections in general. Since it is through the affections that family relations are generally expressed, it comes as no surprise that the strict rationalism of the Kantian and utilitarian schools would view these relations as obstacles to be overcome in the name of reason alone, and as hindrances to the realization of the universal community of rational beings. But the Scottish Enlightenment in fact had a view of the human moral agent that properly takes into account the biological and affectional embeddedness of common human experience.

Thus did Adam Ferguson write in 1792 that moral theory must consider "the scenes in which we find ourselves destined to act." Ferguson underscored the moral value of "natural affections," "instinctive attachments," and the "relations of consanguinity." This moral value stems from the benefits of family duties for society: "Families may be considered as the elementary forms of society, or establishments the most indispensably necessary to the existence and preservation of the kind."[26] Adam Smith, who taught moral philosophy at the University of Glasgow, included a section entitled "Of the Order in which Individuals are recommended by Nature to our care and attention" in his *Theory of Moral Sentiments*. He gives priority to parental affections, and claims that duties to children outweigh those to one's own parents, or to brothers and sisters.[27] He then turns attention to "the poor and the wretched" as follows:

> After the persons who are recommended to our beneficence, either by their connection with ourselves, by their personal qualities, or by their past services, comes those who are pointed out, not indeed to, what is called, our friendship, but to our benevolent attention and good offices; those who are distinguished by their extraordinary situation; the greatly fortunate and the greatly unfortunate, the rich and the powerful, the poor and the wretched.[28]

Moving on to the spheres of neighborhood and country, Smith is rather skeptical about "universal benevolence," since human beings, unlike God, have "narrowness of comprehension," "weakness of powers," and a "much humbler" set of duties.[29] Smith thus discredited those who contemplate the verities of universal sympathy while ignoring the "active duty" to those in proximity, for whom by divine providence duties are ordered. It is not that he thought universal benevolence unimportant, but only that no mere human could ever truly realize the universal. All persons are situated in time and proximity.

Consistent with the Scottish tradition, Alisdair MacIntyre has complained about the "abstract and ghostly" theory of the self characteristic of Kant, and of the Enlightenment in general. He writes: "I am brother, cousin and grandson, member of this household, that village, this tribe. These are not characteristics that belong to human beings accidentally, to be stripped away in order to discover the 'real me.' They are part of my substance, defining partially at least and sometimes wholly my obligations and duties."[30] The self is, phenomenologically considered, essentially immersed and morally bound by particular relations; moreover, these relations should not be overlooked, as if from the moral point of view only universal benevolence counted for goodness.

Ethics is more than what goes on between strangers, between people we see once and will likely never see again. To take away all distinctions of preference based on family relations or loyalties resulting from relationships over time is to strip the moral domain of those areas that are especially valuable. But as Max Scheler, writing in 1915, warned of the social philosophers of his time, "Looking away from oneself is here mistaken for love!" Finally, "all love for a part of mankind—nation, family, individual—now appears as an unjust *deprivation* of what we owe only to the totality." Scheler contrasts "love of mankind" with "love of one's neighbor," which is directed personally at near and visible others. He is critical of Bentham's simplistic notion that "each individual should count for one," as though ethics can be adequately grasped by a form of beneficence "only interested in the *sum total* of human individu-

142

als." Scheler concludes that modern ethics makes concern with proximate persons appear "*a priori* as a *deprivation* of the rights due to the wider circle."[31]

Psychoanalysis and Ethics

Inattention to the order of love with respect to both beneficence and justice greatly concerned Sigmund Freud. Ernest Wallwork's *Psychoanalysis and Ethics* is a splendid study of Freud as ethicist. Wallwork draws his interpretation of Freud chiefly from *Civilization and Its Discontents,* but also from *Group Psychology and the Analysis of the Ego.* Wallwork perceptively includes the following qualification in a footnote:

> Because Freud's target is the common understanding among lay Christians, it is thus not surprising that the ethical writings of at least some theological ethicists generally escape his criticisms: for example, Aquinas recognizes that neighbor love should include the self, and that universal love of humankind is impossible if it is interpreted as requiring the same kind of affection for everyone. (*Summa Theologiae,* II–II, Q. 25, art. iv. and viii). Additionally, Aquinas maintains, as does Freud, that we ought to love our near ones more than others (*Summa Theologiae,* II–II, Q. 26, art. vi).[32]

(Freud's criticisms of the love commandment would convincingly apply to the writings of Kierkegaard and Anders Nygren, among others, who pay scant attention to so-called "special relations," and for whom the embeddedness of the moral agent in biological ordering, in inevitably partial relationships, and in time itself seems to be irrelevant.)

Of Freud's objections to the love commandment, I will concentrate on what Wallwork calls "The Unfairness of Equal Universal Love." "Freud's second major objection to the love commandment," writes Wallwork, "is the predominantly ethical claim that even if we could manage to love a complete stanger equally with an intimate, it would be 'wrong to do so' (SE 21 [1930]: 109)."[33]

Wallwork notes that Freud took seriously the duties imposed by special relations and by the norm of reciprocity. Familial relations and friendships have a certain priority within the domain of love, and they require no apologetics. But the love commandment, as Freud understood it, "counsels promiscuity," Wallwork adds.[34] If special relations are afforded their necessary position in an order of love, then neighbor love becomes less morally simplistic and abstract, as Freud suggests.

Wallwork is quite sympathetic with Freud's critique, since moral prescriptions should be shaped by psychological possibilities. Both selflessness and a reluctance to consider "the priority and distinctive nature of obligations in special relation" are of concern to Wallwork.[35] Finally, he points out that Freud often treated patients who could not afford care, and was generous with time and money: "That Freud's apparent repudiation of the love commandment is actually a reinterpretation of it along more modest lines is indicated by his explicit embrace of an ethic of universal love."[36] I conclude from Wallwork's exposition that Freud certainly allowed for a universal love, but one that takes seriously the structures and psychology of the human self.

Freud rejected the view that human beings lead a shadowlike existence amid principles, as though the moral life is by definition impersonal. His inductive and realist approach to beneficence seriously grapples with the boundaries between the near and distant domains. The fact is that most people struggle to balance obligations to strangers with obligations to family members and friends, as Wallwork suggests Freud himself did. Moreover, they confront difficult moral choices between obligations to self, children, aging parents, spouse, and siblings. Theories of ethics need to say more about how these competing obligations should be morally resolved. Partly influenced by Freud, Don S. Browning writes that "equal-regard does not mean that we should sacrifice the needs of our own children or spouse in an effort ourselves to meet immediately and directly the needs of all other children and all other spouses." Browning argues that the order of beneficence is grounded in commitments and relations that are "necessities of life."[37] He develops a recovery of the *ordo caritatis* through the social sciences, and psychology in particular, while noting that the question of order has not been of interest to most modern ethics.

I have attempted to clarify some of the underlying reasons for the exclusion of family relations from most modern philosophical theories of beneficence and justice. They are mostly based on an underlying philosophy of the self. Looking back, the last discussion of familial ethics in relation to beneficence was that of Sidgwick. I have not tried to provide a systematic position on the interface between family duties and beneficence or distributive justice, or to detail the priorities of the order of beneficence. My less ambitious effort has been to point out the remarkable absence of thought on this matter, a fact mainly attributable to the Enlightenment views of the self and of the moral domain.

A Literary Conclusion

This chapter began with a consideration of several literary works, to which one can be added in conclusion. Dostoevsky, in his *The Brothers Karamazov*, describes an encounter between the old monk Zosima and Mrs. Khokhlakov, who struggles to love those around her. Zosima, the exemplar of love for the stranger, listens attentively. Mrs. Khokhlakov eloquently proclaims her love for humanity, but confesses an inability to actively love others because of their ingratitude or rudeness. In the name of love for humanity, she even contemplates abandoning her daughter. Zosima, in response, recalls a physician who once confessed, "I love mankind but I find to my amazement that the more I love mankind as a whole, the less I love individual people." In his thoughts the physician visualizes potential sacrifices for mankind, but admits that "in actual fact, however, I cannot bear to spend two days in the same room with another person." Moreover, confesses the physician, "Within twenty-four hours I can come to hate the best of men, perhaps because he eats too slowly or because he has a cold and keeps blowing his nose." So to Mrs. Khokhlakov, Zosima concludes: "A true act of love, unlike imaginary love, is hard and forbidding. Imaginary love yearns for an immediate heroic act that is achieved quickly and seen by everyone."[38]

So how shall we balance love for those who are near and dear with love for strangers? The first sphere of love is the one where our natural sympathies lie. The moral life does not require that we trample on these sympathies. On the contrary, it must build on them. Theology does this by telling the story of familial love writ large under a God whose love is parental toward everyone and who makes us all brothers and sisters in sibling solicitude. To love the stranger is an act of filial love as well. The chief task of ethics and all higher religions is to extend human sympathy and solicitude to the stranger. I consider religion at its best to be the most successful source of this extension to the stranger, because people will accomplish things that they believe to be divine will more readily than things they believe to be merely human imperatives.

Notes

1

Introduction: Love Familial and Universal

1. For a useful history of moral philosophy that supports the assertion that current thought is lacking in concern with the family, see Jeffrey Blustein, *Parents and Children: The Ethics of the Family* (New York: Oxford University Press, 1982).

2. See Anders Nygren, *Agape and Eros,* trans. by Philip S. Watson (Chicago: University of Chicago Press, 1982 [original 1938]); Reinhold Niebuhr, *The Nature and Destiny of Man* (New York: Charles Scribner's Sons, 1941).

3. Amitai Etzioni, *The Spirit of Community: Rights, Responsibilities, and the Communitarian Agenda* (New York: Crown, 1993).

4. David Popenoe, *Disturbing the Nest: Family Change in Modern Societies* (Hawthorne, N.Y.: Aldine de Gruyter, 1988).

5. See the National Commission on Children, *Beyond Rhetoric: A New American Agenda for Children and Families* (Washington, D.C.: U.S. Government Printing Office, 1991).

6. Ibid., p. 251.

7. Alan Donagan, *The Theory of Morality* (Chicago: University of Chicago Press, 1977), p. 101.

8. Stephanie Coontz, *The Way We Never Were: American Families and the Nostalgia Trap* (New York: Basic Books, 1992), p. 36.

9. Garth L. Hallett, *Christian Neighbor-Love: An Assessment of Six Rival Versions* (Georgetown: Georgetown University Press, 1989).

10. William James, *The Varieties of Religious Experience* (New York: Collier Books, 1961 [original 1902]).

11. Edith Wyschogrod, *Saints and Postmodernism* (Chicago: University of Chicago Press, 1990).

12. See Jeffrey Blustein, *Care and Commitment: Taking the Personal Point of View* (New York: Oxford University Press, 1991), Introduction.

13. Nicolai Hartmann, *Ethics,* vol. 2, trans. by Stanton Coit (New York: George Allen & Unwin, Ltd., 1932).

14. Bernard Williams, "A Critique of Utilitarianism," in *Utilitarianism: For and Against,* ed. by J. J. C. Smart and Bernard Williams (Cambridge: Cambridge University Press, 1973).

15. See Stephen J. Pope, *The Evolution of Altruism and the Ordering of Love* Washington, D.C.: Georgetown University Press, 1994.

16. Sally B. Purvis, "Mothers, Neighbors, and Strangers: Another Look at Agape," *Journal of Feminist Studies in Religion* 7, no. 1 (1991), p. 19.

17. Gilbert Meilaender, *The Limits of Love: Some Theological Explorations* (University Park, Pa.: The Pennsylvania State University Press, 1987), p. 22.

18. Stephen G. Post, *A Theory of Agape: On the Meaning of Christian Love* (Lewisburg, Pa.: Bucknell University Press; London and Toronto: Associated University Presses, 1990).

19. Paul J. Wadell, *Friendship* (Notre Dame: University of Notre Dame Press, 1990).

20. See Stanley Hauerwas, *The Peaceable Kingdom* (Notre Dame: University of Notre Dame Press, 1983).

21. Gilbert C. Meilaender, *Friendship: A Study in Theological Ethics* (Notre Dame: University of Notre Dame Press, 1981).

22. Catherine Keller, "Feminism and the Ethic of Inseparability," in *Women's Consciousness and Women's Conscience,* ed. by Barbara Hilkert Andolsen, Christine E. Gudorf, and Mary D. Pellauer (San Francisco: Harper & Row, 1985), pp. 1–46.

23. Susan Moller Okin, *Justice, Gender, and the Family* (New York: Basic Books, 1989).

24. James M. Gustafson, *Ethics from a Theocentric Perspective,* vol. 2: *Ethics and Theology* (Chicago: University of Chicago Press, 1984), p. 165.

25. Immanuel Kant, "Duties toward the Body in Respect of Sexual Impulse," in *Lectures on Ethics,* trans. by Louis Infield (Indianapolis: Hackett Publishing, 1963 [original 1780]), p. 163.

26. See Nancy R. Gibbs, "Bringing Up Father," *Time* 141, no. 26 (28 June 1993), pp. 53–61.

27. There is now a growing literature in men's studies on fatherly love. See Frank Pittman, *Man Enough: Fathers, Sons, and the Search for Masculinity* (New York: G. P. Putnam's Sons, 1993); Richard Louv, *Fatherlove* (New York: Simon & Schuster, 1993); and Arthur D. and Libby D. Coleman, *The Father* (New York: Avon Books, 1988).

28. Albert Camus, *The Fall,* trans. by Justin O'Brien (New York: Vintage Books, 1991 [original 1957]). See chapter 8 for further discussion of this book.

29. Sissela Bok, *A Strategy for Peace: Human Values and the Threat of War* (New York: Vintage, 1990), p. 178, n. 6.

30. E. P. Sanders, *Jesus and Judaism* (Philadelphia: Fortress Press, 1985), p. 146.

31. Ibid., p. 319.

32. Ibid., p. 257.

33. Ibid., pp. 233–234.

34. Ibid., p. 260.

2

Married Love

1. Amitai Etzioni, *The Spirit of Community: Rights, Responsibilities, and the Communitarian Agenda* (New York: Crown, 1993), p. 77.

2. An excellent recent study is Susan A. Ross, "The Bride of Christ and the Body Politic: Body and Gender in Pre-Vatican II Marriage Theology," *Journal of Religion* 71, no. 3 (July 1991), pp. 345–361.

3. Edward S. Gleason, *Redeeming Marriage* (Cambridge, Mass.: Cowley Publishers, 1988).

4. Etzioni, *The Spirit of Community,* p. 78.

5. Philip Turner, *Sexual Ethics and the Attack on Traditional Morality* (New York: Forward Movement Publishers, 1988), p.17. See also Turner's *Sex, Money and Power* (Cambridge, Mass.: Cowley Publications, 1985), p. 17.

6. Geoffrey Parrinder, *Sex in the World's Religions* (New York: Oxford, 1980), p. 208.

7. R. Newton Flew, *The Idea of Perfection in Christian Theology: An Historical Study of the Christian Ideal for the Present Life* (New York: Humanities Press, 1968). See also John Passmore, *The Perfectibility of Man* (New York: Charles Scribner's Sons, 1970), which covers the entire history of the idea of human perfection.

8. See Sallie McFague, *Models of God: Theology for an Ecological Nuclear Age* (Philadelphia: Fortress Press, 1987); also Elisabeth Moltmann-Wendel and Jurgen Moltmann, *Humanity in God* (Cleveland, Ohio: Pilgrim Press, 1983).

9. Martin Luther, "The Estate of Marriage," *Luther's Works,* vol. 45: *Christian in Society, Vol. II,* ed. by Walther I. Brandt (Philadelphia: Fortress Press, 1962), pp. 17–49.

10. Elisabeth S. Fiorenza, *In Memory of Her* (New York: Crossroad, 1984); also, Hans Dieter Betz, *Galatians* (Philadelphia: Fortress Press, 1979).

11. Emil Brunner, *The Divine Imperative,* trans. by Olive Wyon (Philadelphia: Westminster Press, 1937), pp. 345, 346.

12. Cited in Richard D. Klyver, *Brother James: The Life and Times of Shaker Elder, James Prescott* (Solon, Ohio: The Evans Printing Co., 1992), p. 164.

13. William Temple, *Nature, God and Man* (New York: Macmillan, 1949), p. 226.

14. Cecil John Cadoux, *The Early Church and the World* (Edinburgh: T. & T. Clark, 1925), p. 60.

15. Ibid., p. 124.

16. Barbara E. Reed, "Taoism," in *Women in World Religions,* ed. by Arvind Sharma (Albany: State University of New York Press, 1987), pp. 165, 166.

17. Virginia Ramey Mollenkott, *Women, Men, and the Bible* (Nashville: Abingdon Press, 1977); see also her *The Divine Feminine: The Biblical Imagery of God as Female* (New York: Crossroad, 1991).

18. Elaine H. Pagels, "What Became of God the Mother? Conflicting Images of God in Early Christianity," in *Womanspirit Rising: A Feminist Reader in Religion,* ed. by Carol P. Christ and Judith Plaskow (New York: Harper & Row, 1979), p. 110.

19. Phyllis Trible, *God and the Rhetoric of Sexuality* (Philadelphia: Fortress Press, 1978).

20. Mollenkott, *The Divine Feminine,* pp. 13, 116.

21. Linda A. Mercadante, *Gender, Doctrine and God: The Shakers and Contemporary Theology* (Nashville: Abingdon Press, 1990), p. 85.

22. Francis Wayland, *The Elements of Moral Science,* ed. by Joseph L. Blau (Cambridge, Mass.: Harvard University Press, 1963 [original 1835]), p. 279.

23. Denis de Rougemont, *Love in the Western World,* trans. by Montgomery Belgion (New York: Harper Colophon Books, 1974 [original 1940]), p. 279.

24. See Elaine Hatfield, "Passionate and Companionate Love," in *The Psychology of Love,* ed. by Robert J. Sternberg and Michael L. Barnes (New Haven: Yale University Press, 1988), pp. 191–217.

25. Susan Moller Okin, *Justice, Gender, and the Family* (New York: Basic Books, 1989).

26. Lisa Sowle Cahill, *Between the Sexes: Foundations for a Christian Ethics of Sexuality* (New York: Paulist Press, 1985), p. 99.

27. Margaret A. Farley, *Personal Commitments* (San Francisco: Harper & Row, 1986).

28. An excellent overview of early Christian attitudes toward marriage is David G. Hunter, ed., *Marriage in the Early Church* (Minneapolis: Augsburg/Fortress Press, 1992).

29. Stanley Hauerwas, "The Family: Theological Reflections," *A Community of Character: Toward a Constructive Christian Social Ethics* (Notre Dame: University of Notre Dame Press, 1981), p. 172.

30. Marie-Henry Beyle Stendahl, "The Crystallizations of Passion-Love," in *Philosophies of Love,* ed. by David L. Norton and Mary F. Kille (Totowa, N.J.: Rowman & Allanheld, 1971), pp. 32–41.

31. Georges Duby, *The Knight, The Lady, and the Priest: The Making of Modern Marriage in Medieval France,* trans. by Barbara Bray (New York: Pantheon, 1983), p. 162.

32. James M. Gustafson, *Ethics and Theology,* vol. 2 of *Ethics from a Theocentric Perspective* (Chicago: University of Chicago Press, 1984), pp. 159, 98.

33. Roger Mehl, *Society and Love: Ethical Problems in Family Life,* trans. by James H. Farley (Philadelphia: Westminster Press, 1964).

34. Walter Rauschenbusch, *Dare We Be Christians?* (Boston: Pilgrim Press, 1914), p. 29–32.

35. Ibid., p. 30.

36. Daniel Day Williams, *The Spirit and the Forms of Love* (New York: Harper & Row, 1968), p. 232.

3
The Misuse of Sexual Love

1. Max Scheler, *On the Eternal in Man,* trans. by B. Noble (London: SCM Press, 1960 [original 1921]), p. 367.

2. Willard Gaylin, *Rediscovering Love* (New York: Penguin, 1986), p. 11.

3. Steven Seidman, *Embattled Eros: Sexual Politics and Ethics in Contemporary America* (New York: Routledge, 1992), p. 10.

4. Paul R. Fleishman, *The Healing Zone: Religious Issues in Psychotherapy* (New York: Paragon House, 1989), p. 173.

5. Ibid., p. 174.

6. Rollo May, *Love and Will* (New York: Dell Publishing, 1969), p. 42.

7. John D'Emilio and Estelle B. Freedman, *Intimate Matters: A History of Sexuality in America* (New York: Harper & Row, 1988), pp. 223, 225.

8. C. S. Lewis, *Mere Christianity* (New York: Macmillan, 1952), pp. 78, 81.

9. Gabrielle Brown, *The New Celibacy: A Journey of Love, Intimacy, and Good Health in a New Age,* 2nd ed. (New York: McGraw-Hill, 1989), p. 18.

10. Catherine A. MacKinnon, *Toward a Feminist Theory of the State* (Cambridge, Mass.: Harvard University Press, 1989).

11. Michel Foucault, *The History of Sexuality,* vol. III: *The Care of the Self,* trans. by Robert Hurley (New York: Vintage Books, 1988).

12. James B. Nelson, *Embodiment: An Approach to Sexuality and Christian Theology* (Minneapolis: Augsburg, 1979).

13. Christopher Dawson, *Progress and Religion* (Garden City, N.Y.: Doubleday & Co., 1960), p. 181.

14. Søren Kierkegaard, *The Concept of Anxiety: A Simple Psychologically Orienting Deliberation on the Dogmatic Issue of Hereditary Sin,* trans. by R. Thomte (Princeton, N.J.: Princeton University Press, 1980 [original 1844]), p. 80.

15. Immanuel Kant, "Duties toward the Body in Respect of Sexual Impulse," in *Lectures on Ethics,* trans. by Louis Infield (Indianapolis: Hackett Publishing Co., 1963), p. 163.

16. Jean Danielou, *In the Beginning* (Baltimore: Helicon Press, 1965), p. 54.

17. Reinhold Niebuhr, *The Nature and Destiny of Man,* vol. 1: *Human Nature* (New York: Charles Scribner's Sons, 1941), p. 235.

18. Space will not allow a full review of these perspectives. I am aware of the vast literature on Kierkegaard's view of the Fall. Gregor Maluntschuk, in *Kierkegaard's Thought* (Princeton, N.J.: Princeton University Press, 1971), makes the important point that in *The Concept of Anxiety* Kierkegaard deals with sin from a psychological perspective. George Stack, in *Kierkegaard's Existential Ethics* (Birmingham: University of Alabama Press, 1976), argues that the notion of sin belongs exclusively to the religious stage of existence (pp. 132–133). Among the many other significant discussions are these: James Collins, *The Mind of Kierkegaard* (Princeton, N.J.: Princeton University Press, 1983), pp. 221–222; Louis K. Dupre, *Kierkegaard as Theologian* (New York: Sheed & Ward, 1963), pp. 49–62; Robert L. Perkins, *Soren Kierkegaard* (Richmond: John Knox Press, 1969), pp. 26–29; George Price, *The Narrow Pass: Kierkegaard's Concept of Man* (New York: McGraw-Hill, 1963), pp. 45–51.

19. Kierkegaard, *The Concept of Anxiety,* p. 80.

20. Ibid., pp. 69, 79, 77.

21. Ibid., p. 63.

22. Ibid., pp. 58, 70.

23. Elaine Pagels, *Adam, Eve, and the Serpent* (New York: Vintage Books, 1988), p. xix.

24. Ibid., pp. 18, 19.

25. Ibid., p. 21.

26. Ibid., p. 27.

27. Ibid., p. 28; emphasis mine.

28. Parenthetically, my preference is for the Irenaean interpretation, in which Adam and Eve never achieved the condition of spiritual maturity with respect to both love for God and for neighbor but instead fell into a premature sexual intimacy, i.e., an intimacy not qualified by spirit and profound love.

29. Gilbert Meilaender, *The Limits of Love: Some Theological Explorations* (University Park, Pa.: The Pennsylvania State University Press, 1987), p. 116.

30. Nelson, *Embodiment,* pp. 35, 41, 45, 105.

31. Meilaender, *The Limits of Love,* pp. 117, 118.

32. James B. Nelson, *The Intimate Connection: Male Sexuality, Male Spirituality* (Philadelphia: Westminster Press, 1988).

33. Nelson, *Embodiment,* p. 149.

34. Daniel Day Williams, *The Spirit and the Forms of Love* (New York: Harper & Row, 1968), pp. 227, 236, 237.

35. Gerhard von Rad, *Genesis* (London: SCM Press, 1956), p. 58.

36. For a powerful feminist critique of Jewish patriarchy, see Judith Plaskow, *Standing Again at Sinai: Judaism from a Feminist Perspective* (San Francisco: Harper & Row, 1990).

37. Martin Luther, "The Estate of Marriage," *Luther's Works,* vol. 45: *The Christian in Society, Vol. II,* ed. by Walther I. Brandt (Philadelphia: Fortress, 1962), p. 49.

4

Parental Love

1. Sallie McFague, "Mother God," in *Motherhood: Experience, Institutions, Theology,* ed. by Ann Carr and Elizabeth Schussler Fiorenza (Edinburgh: T. & T. Clark, 1989), pp. 139, 140 (emphasis in original).

2. Amitai Etzioni, *The Spirit of Community: Rights, Responsibilities, and the Communitarian Agenda* (New York: Crown Publishers, 1993), p. 54.

3. The National Commission on Children, *Beyond Rhetoric: A New American Agenda for Children and Families* (Washington, D.C.: U.S. Government Printing Offices, 1991), pp. 66, 68.

4. Etzioni, *The Spirit of Community,* p. 70.

5. Barbara Dafoe Whitehead, "The New Family Values," *Utne Reader,* no. 57 (May/June 1993), pp. 65, 66.

6. Susan Moller Okin, *Justice, Gender, and the Family* (New York: Basic Books, 1989), p. 39.

7. Larry May and Robert Strikwerda, "Fatherhood and Nurturance," *Journal of Social Philosophy* 22, no. 2 (Fall 1991), p. 39.

8. Mary Francis Berry, *The Politics of Parenthood: Child Care, Women's Rights and the Myth of the Good Mother* (New York: Viking, 1993), p. 42.

9. Ibid., pp. 42–47.

10. David Popenoe, "Fostering the New Familism," *The Responsive Community: Rights and Responsibilities* 2, no. 4 (Fall 1992), p. 35.

11. Stephanie Coontz, *The Way We Never Were: American Families and the Nostalgia Trap* (New York: Basic Books, 1992).

12. Popenoe, "Fostering the New Familism," p. 33.

13. The National Center for Health Statistics, *Vital Statistics of the United States,* annual and *Monthly Vital Statistics Report,* vol. 41, no. 9 supplement, February 25, 1993. On teen pregnancy and the related problem of welfare dependency, see David A. Hamburg, M.D., *Today's Children: Creating a Future for a Generation in Crisis* (New York: Random House, 1992), p. 198.

14. See the summary of the National Health Interview Survey in Deborah A. Dawson, "Family Structure and Children's Health and Well Being: Data from the 1988 National Interview Survey on Child Care," *Journal of Marriage and the Family* 53 (1991), pp. 573–584.

15. See Sara McLanahan and Gary Sandefur, *Uncertain Childhood, Uncertain Future: Growing Up with a Single Parent* (Cambridge, Mass.: Harvard University Press, 1994).

16. Dawson, "Family Structure and Children's Health."

17. David Popenoe, *Disturbing the Nest: Family Change and Decline in Modern Societies* (Hawthorne, N.Y.: Aldine de Gruyter, 1988), pp. 302, 305.

18. John Locke, *The Second Treatise of Government,* ed. by Thomas P. Peardon (Indianapolis: Bobbs-Merrill, 1952 [original 1690]).

19. Robert Filmer, *Patriarcha and Other Political Works,* ed. by Peter Laslett (Oxford: Basil Blackwell, 1949), p. 57.

20. Michael A. Slote, "Obedience and Illusions," in *Having Children: Philosophical and Legal Reflections on Parenthood,* ed. by Onora O'Neill and William Ruddick (New York: Oxford University Press, 1979) pp. 319–326.

21. Ivone Gebara, "The Mother Superior and Spiritual Motherhood: From Intuition to Institution," in *Motherhood: Experience, Institutions, Theology,* p. 48.

22. Sallie McFague, *Models of God: Theology for an Ecological Nuclear Age* (Philadelphia: Fortress Press, 1987), pp. 103, 119, 121.

23. A classic expression of this concern in theological ethics is Valerie Saving, "The Human Situation," in *Womanspirit Rising,* ed. by Carol Christ and Judith Plaskow (New York: Harper & Row, 1979), pp. 25–42. Another very useful summary is Barbara H. Andolsen, "Agape in Feminist Ethics," *Journal of Religious Ethics* 9, no. 1 (Spring 1981), pp. 69–83. See also Adrienne Rich, *Of Woman Born: Motherhood as Experience and Institution* (New York: W. W. Norton, 1986).

24. Jeffner Allen, "Motherhood: The Annihilation of Women," in *Mothering: Essays in Feminist Theory,* ed. by Joyce Trebilcot (Savage, Md.: Rowman & Littlefield, 1983), p. 315. This Trebilcot collection contains a variety of other powerful antinatalist chapters.

25. Margaret Farley, *Personal Commitments: Beginning, Keeping, Changing* (San Francisco: Harper & Row, 1986), pp. 80–81.

26. Stanley Hauerwas, *A Community of Character: Toward a Constructive Christian Social Ethic* (Notre Dame: University of Notre Dame Press, 1981), p. 173.

27. John Benson, "Duty and the Beast," *Philosophy: The Journal of the Royal Institute of Philosophy* 53, no. 206 (October 1978), p. 536.

28. Daniel Day Williams, *The Spirit and the Forms of Love* (New York: Harper & Row, 1968), p. 122.

29. Paul Ramsey, *Fabricated Man: The Ethics of Genetic Control* (New Haven: Yale University Press, 1970), p. 38.

30. Emil Brunner, *The Divine Imperative,* trans. by Olive Wyon (Philadelphia: Westminster Press, 1937), p. 346.

31. Ibid., p. 346.

32. John Burnaby, *Amor Dei: A Study in the Religion of St. Augustine* (London: Hodder & Stoughton, 1938), p. 302.

33. Marie-Theres Wacker, "God as Mother? On the Meaning of a Biblical God-symbol for Feminist Theology," in *Motherhood: Experience, Institution, Theology,* p. 105.

34. See Abraham J. Heschel, *God in Search of Man* (New York: Free Press, 1959).

35. Abraham Heschel, *The Prophets,* 2 vols. (New York: Harper & Row, 1962).

36. This definition of *storge* is taken from C. S. Lewis, *The Four Loves* (New York: Harcourt Brace Jovanovich, 1960), p. 53.

37. Willard Gaylin, *Adam and Eve and Pinocchio: On Being and Becoming Human* (New York: Viking, 1990), p. 214.

38. Karl Barth discusses this role in "Parents and Children," *Church Dogmatics,* vol. 3, pt. 4, ed. by G. W. Bromiley and T. F. Torrence (Edinburgh: T. & T. Clark, 1961).

39. Robert Jay Lifton, *The Nazi Doctors* (New York: Basic Books,

1986); and (with Eric Markusen), *The Genocidal Mentality: Nazi Holocaust and Nuclear Threat* (New York: Basic Books, 1988).

40. Sally B. Purvis, "Mothers, Neighbors, and Strangers: Another Look as Agape," *Journal of Feminist Studies in Religion* 7, no. 1 (1991), p. 19.

41. Jonathan Edwards, *The Nature of True Virtue,* with a Foreword by William K. Frankena (Ann Arbor, Michigan: University of Michigan Press, 1960 [original 1755]), p. 76.

42. Virginia Held, "Feminism and Moral Theory," in Eva Feder Kittay and Diana T. Meyers, eds., *Women and Moral Theory* (Totowa, N.J.: Rowman and Allanheld, 1987), p. 118.

43. Ibid., p. 118.

44. Sara Ruddick, *Maternal Thinking: Toward a Politics of Peace* (Boston: Beacon Press, 1989), pp. 15, 42.

45. A feminist study on motherhood and medical technology is Barbara Katz Rothman, *Recreating Motherhood: Ideology and Technology in a Patriarchal Society* (New York: W. W. Norton, 1989).

46. Joseph L. Allen, *Love and Conflict: A Covenantal Model of Christian Ethics* (Nashville: Abingdon Press, 1984), pp. 34, 41, 45.

47. Norman L. Geisler, *The Christian Ethics of Love* (Grand Rapids, Mich.: Zondervan Publishing House, 1973), p. 37.

48. Louis Colin, C.S.S.R., *Love One Another,* trans. by Fergus Murphy (Westminster, Md.: The Newman Press, 1960), pp. 175–176.

49. Ibid., pp. 176, 178.

50. See Okin, *Justice, Gender, and the Family.*

51. John Paul II, *Familiaris Consortio* (Washington, D.C.: United States Catholic Conference, 1981), pp. 21, 41.

52. Henri Bergson, *The Two Sources of Morality and Religion,* trans. by R. Audra (Garden City, N.Y.: Doubleday, 1935), p. 34.

53. Paul Tillich, *Love, Power, and Justice* (New York: Oxford University Press, 1954), p. 116.

54. Ibid., p. 119.

5

Filial Love

1. John Burnaby, *Amor Dei: A Study of the Religion of St. Augustine* (London: Hodder & Stoughton, 1938), p. 302 (emphasis in original).

2. Daniel Mark Epstein, *Love's Compass: A Natural History of the Heart* (Reading, Mass.: Addison-Wesley, 1990), pp. 16, 41.

3. Nel Noddings, *Caring: A Feminine Approach to Ethics and Moral Education* (Berkeley: University of California Press, 1984), p. 5.

4. Ibid., p. 59.

5. Morton T. Kelsey, *Caring: How Can We Love One Another?* (New York: Paulist Press, 1981), p. 87.

6. See Robert Jay Lifton, *The Nazi Doctors* (New York: Basic Books, 1986).

7. Henri J. M. Nouwen, *The Return of the Prodigal Son: A Meditation on Fathers, Brothers, and Sons* (New York: Doubleday, 1992),p. 90.

8. Ibid., p. 94.

9. Ibid., pp. 94, 102.

10. Dorothy Emmet, *The Nature of Metaphysical Thinking* (New York: St. Martin's Press, 1945), p. 6.

11. See Douglas S. Diekema, "Metaphor, Medicine, and Morals," *Soundings,* 72, no.1 (Spring 1989), pp. 17–24.

12. Mark Turner, "Categories and Analogies," in *Analogical Reasoning,* ed. by David H. Helman (Dordrecht: Kluwer Academic Publishers, 1988), pp. 3, 6.

13. William F. May, *The Physician's Covenant: Images of the Healer in Medical Ethics* (Philadelphia: The Westminster Press, 1983), p. 15.

14. See Jacques Maritain, *On the Philosophy of History,* ed. by Joseph W. Evans (New York: Charles Scribner's Sons, 1957), p. 69.

15. John Burnaby, *Amor Dei,* pp. 305, 306.

16. Erich Fromm, *The Art of Loving: An Enquiry into the Nature of Love* (New York: Harper & Row, 1956), p. 40.

17. Daniel Day Williams, *The Spirit and the Forms of Love* (New York: Harper & Row, 1968).

18. Stephen G. Post, "History, Infanticide, and Imperiled Newborns," *Hastings Center Report,* vol. 18, no. 4 (1988), pp. 14–17.

19. James Garbarino, "The Incidence and Prevalence of Child Maltreatment," in *Family Violence,* ed. by Lloyd Ohlin and Michael Tonry (Chicago: University of Chicago Press, 1989), p. 221.

20. Helen Kandel Hyman, "Intergenerational Relationships: Adult Children and Aging Parents," *Affirmative Aging: A Resource for Ministry* (Minneapolis: Winston, 1985), p. 84.

21. Personal correspondence with the author, 1987. D. Lydia Bronte coedited, with Alan Pifer, *Our Aging Society: Paradox and Promise* (New York: Norton, 1986).

22. Cited in Stephen Sapp, *Full of Years* (Nashville: Abingdon Press, 1987), p. 85.

23. Michael A. Slote, "Obedience and Illusion," in *Having Children: Philosphical and Legal Reflections on Parenthood,* pp. 319–326.

24. Jeffrey Blustein, *Parents and Children: The Ethics of the Family* (New York: Oxford University Press, 1982), p. 182.

25. Ibid., pp. 179, 182.

26. Dostoyevsky, *The Adolescent (or A Raw Youth)*. In *The Gospel in Dostoyevsky: Selections from His Works,* ed. by the Hutterite Brethren (Ulster, N.Y.: Plough Publishing House, 1988), p. 219.

27. Ibid., p. 229.

28. Ibid., p. 221.

29. Ibid., p. 226.

30. James F. Childress, *Who Should Decide: Paternalism in Health Care* (New York: Oxford University Press, 1982), p. 42.

31. Sapp, *Full of Years,* pp. 133, 159.

32. Leo W. Simmons, *The Role of the Aged in Primitive Society* (New Haven: Yale University Press, 1945), p. 82.

33. William F. May, "Who Cares for the Elderly?" *Hastings Center Report,* 12, no. 6 (1982), p. 36.

34. Robert N. Butler, *Why Survive? Being Old in America* (New York: Harper & Row, 1975), p. 11.

35. Karl Barth, *The Doctrine of Creation: Church Dogmatics,* vol. 3, pt. 4, trans. by A. T. Mackay (Edinburgh: T. & T. Clark, 1961), pp. 244–245.

36. Ibid., p. 243.

6
Familial Love: Self-Denial and Self-Concern

1. Daniel Callahan, *Setting Limits: Medical Goals in an Aging Society* (New York: Simon & Schuster, 1987), p. 107.

2. Gilbert Meilaender, "I Want to Burden My Loved Ones," *First Things,* no. 16 (October 1991), pp. 12–16.

3. Susan Moller Okin, *Justice, Gender, and the Family* (New York: Basic Books, 1989), p. 4.

4. Garth L. Hallett, *Christian Neighbor-Love: An Assessment of Six Rival Versions* (Washington, D.C.: Georgetown University Press, 1989).

5. Gene Outka, *Agape: An Ethical Analysis* (New Haven: Yale University Press, 1972). Also, Don S. Browning, *Religious Thought and the Modern Psychologies* (Philadelphia: Fortress Press, 1987).

6. Stephen G. Post, "Disinterested Benevolence: An American Debate over the Nature of Christian Love," *Journal of Religious Ethics* 14, no. 2 (Fall 1986), pp. 356–368.

7. James M. Gustafson, *Ethics from a Theocentric Perspective,* vol. 2, *Ethics and Theology* (Chicago: University of Chicago Press, 1984), p. 170.

8. Robert Jay Lifton, *Boundaries* (New York: Vintage Books, 1970).

9. See Robert H. Binstock, Stephen G. Post, and Peter J. Whitehouse, eds., *Dementia and Aging: Ethics, Values, and Policy Choices,* with a Foreword by Robert N. Butler (Baltimore: Johns Hopkins University Press, 1992).

10. Gabriel Marcel, *The Philosophy of Existentialism,* trans. by M. Harari (Secaucus, N.J.: Citadel Press, 1956), pp. 74–75.

11. Robert Bellah et al., *Habits of the Heart: Individualism and Commitment in American Life* (San Francisco: Harper & Row, 1985), ch. 4.

12. J. F. Kennedy, "Maternal Reactions to the Birth of a Defective Baby," *Social Casework* 51 (1970), pp. 98–110.

13. Sandra L. Harris, *Families of the Developmentally Disabled: A Guide to Behavioral Intervention* (New York: Pergamon Press, 1983).

14. Helen Featherstone, *A Difference in the Family: Life with a Disabled Child* (New York: Basic Books, 1980), pp. 19, 35.

15. Rosalyn Darling, *Families against Society* (Beverly Hills: Sage Library of Social Research, 1979), p. 172.

16. James M. Gustafson, "Mongolism, Parental Desires, and the Right to Life," in *Bioethics,* ed. by Thomas A. Shannon (Ramsey, N.J.: Paulist Press, 1981), pp. 154–155.

17. Henry Sidgwick, *The Methods of Ethics* (Indianapolis: Hackett Publishing, 1981 [original 1907]), pp. 259–260.

18. C. S. Lewis, *The Abolition of Man* (New York: Macmillan, 1947), p. 41.

19. Ibid., p. 104.

20. Jane English, "What Do Grown Children Owe Their Parents?" in Onora O'Neill and William Ruddick, eds., *Having Children: Philosophical and Legal Reflections on Parenthood* (New York: Oxford University Press, 1979), p. 351.

21. Everett W. Hall, *Our Knowledge of Fact and Values* (Chapel Hill: University of North Carolina Press, 1961), p. 6.

22. Augustine, *The City of God,* trans. by Marcus Dods (New York: Modern Library, 1950), p. 693.

23. Bernard Haring, *The Law of Christ,* trans. by E. G. Kaiser (Westminster, Md.: Newman Press, 1966), vol. 3, p. 112.

24. Christina Hoff Sommers, "Filial Morality," *Journal of Philosophy* 83, no. 8 (August 1986), p. 439.

25. Stephen G. Post, "Women and Elderly Parents: Moral Controversy in an Aging Society," *Hypatia: A Journal of Feminist Philosophy* 5, no. 1 (Spring 1990), pp. 83–89.

26. The classic theological-ethical statement of this position remains that of Valerie Saiving, "The Human Situation: A Feminine View,"

in *Womanspirit Rising: A Feminist Reader in Religion,* ed. by Carol P. Christ and Judith Plaskow (San Francisco: Harper & Row, 1979), pp. 25–42.

27. Arlene Skolnick and Jerome H. Skolnick, *Family in Transition* (Boston: Little, Brown, 1980), p. 51.

28. This myth is discussed in Kenneth Keniston and the Carnegie Council on Children, *All Our Children: The American Family under Pressure* (New York: Harcourt Brace Jovanovich, 1977).

29. Margaret A. Farley, *Personal Commitments* (San Francisco: Harper & Row, 1986), p. 75.

30. Elaine M. Brody, *Women in the Middle: Their Parent-Care Years* (New York: Springer Publishing, 1990), p. 13.

31. Ibid., 35.

32. Ibid., 42.

7
Love for Strangers

1. Gene Outka, *Agape: An Ethical Analysis* (New Haven: Yale University Press, 1972), pp. 263–267.

2. See the *Didache* and the *Epistle of Barnabus* in *Early Christian Writings,* trans. by Maxwell Staniforth (New York: Penguin, 1968), pp. 227–236 and pp. 193–222.

3. Dewi Z. Phillips, "The Christian Concept of Love," in Ian T. Ramsey, ed., *Christian Ethics and Contemporary Philosophy* (New York: Macmillan, 1966), p. 315.

4. Edith Wyschogrod, *Saints and Postmodernism: Revisioning Moral Philosophy* (Chicago: University of Chicago Press, 1990), p. xiii.

5. See Stanley Hauerwas, *The Peaceable Kingdom: A Primer in Christian Ethics* (Notre Dame: University of Notre Dame Press, 1983).

6. W. E. H. Lecky, *History of European Morals from Augustus to Charlemagne* (New York: George Braziller, 1955).

7. See Paul Ramsey, *Basic Christian Ethics* (Chicago: University of Chicago reprint, 1978), ch. 7.

8. Owsei Temkin, *Hippocrates in a World of Pagans and Christians* (Baltimore: Johns Hopkins University Press, 1991), p. 32.

9. John Ferguson, *Moral Values in the Ancient World* (New York: Barnes & Noble, 1959).

10. Henry Sigerist, *Civilization and Disease* (Ithaca: Cornell University Press, 1943).

11. Wyschogrod, *Saints and Postmodernism.*

12. Robert Wuthnow, *Acts of Compassion: Caring for Others and Helping Ourselves* (Princeton: Princeton University Press, 1991).

13. Alan Soble, *The Structure of Love* (New Haven: Yale University Press, 1990) p. 15.

14. See Irving Singer, *The Nature of Love: The Modern World* (Chicago: University of Chicago Press, 1987).

15. See Robert Hazo, *The Idea of Love* (New York: Praeger, 1967).

16. Soren Kierkegaard, *Works of Love,* trans. by Howard and Edna Hong (Princeton: Princeton University Press, 1962 [original 1857]).

17. John M. Rist, "Some Interpretations of Agape and Eros," in Charles W. Kegley, ed., *The Philosophy and Theology of Anders Nygren* (Carbondale, Ill.: Southern Illinois University Press, 1970), p. 163.

18. Anders Nygren, *Agape and Eros,* trans. by Phillip S. Watson (Chicago: University of Chicago reprint, 1982), p. 68.

19. Ibid., pp. 82–91.

20. Martin C. D'Arcy, *The Mind and Heart of Love* (Cleveland: World Publishing, 1956), p. 82.

21. Rist, "Some Interpretations," pp. 169, 168.

22. D'Arcy, *The Mind and Heart of Love,* pp. 90, 83.

23. Karl Barth, *Church Dogmatics,* vol. 4, pt. 2, trans. by G. W. Bromily (Edinburgh: T.& T. Clark, 1958), pp. 807, 804.

24. Ibid., p. 808.

25. Nygren, *Agape and Eros,* p. 154.

26. Rist, "Some Interpretations," p. 169.

27. Barth, *Church Dogmatics,* vol. 4, pt. 2, p. 802.

28. Outka, *Agape,* pp. 211–212.

29. Gene Outka, "Social Justice and Equal Access to Health Care," *Journal of Religious Ethics* 2 (1974), pp. 11–32.

30. Jack T. Sanders, *Ethics in the New Testament: Change and Development* (Philadelphia: Fortress Press, 1975), p. 95.

31. Helen Oppenheimer, *The Hope of Happiness: A Sketch for a Christian Humanism* (London: SCM Press, 1983), p. 113.

32. Ibid., pp. 112, 113.

33. Rist, "Some Interpretations," p. 173.

34. Richard Swinburne, *Responsibility and Atonement* (New York: Oxford University Press, 1989), p. 81.

35. Ibid., pp. 82, 86, 163.

36. Warren McWilliams, *The Passion of God: Divine Suffering in Contemporary Protestant Thought* (Macon, Ga.: Mercer University Press, 1985).

37. Martin Buber, *I and Thou* (New York: Scribner's, 1958). See Maurice S. Friedman, *Martin Buber: The Life of Dialogue* (New York: Harper & Row, 1960).

38. Oppenheimer, *The Hope of Happiness,* pp. 111–112.

39. Buber, *I and Thou,* p. 82.

40. Victor Paul Furnish provides a detailed analysis of the usage of different words for love in his *The Love Command in the New Testament* (Nashville: Abingdon Press, 1972).

41. Paul J. Wadell, *Friendship and the Moral Life* (Notre Dame: University of Notre Dame Press, 1989), p. xiii.

42. Ibid., p. 5.

43. Ibid., p. 70.

44. Ibid., p. 73 (emphasis mine)

45. Ibid., p. 74.

8
An Order of Love: Close Ties and Strangers

1. Louis Janssens, "Norms and Priorities in a Love Ethics," *Louvain Studies* 6 (1977), p. 212.

2. See Stephen J. Pope, "The Order of Love, and Recent Catholic Ethics: A Constructive Proposal," *Theological Studies* 52, no. 2 (June 1991), pp. 255–288. This is an excellent criticism of recent Catholic ethics for failing to attend sufficiently to the ordering of love. Pope develops his recovery of Aquinas through the insights of certain aspects of sociobiology. See also Pope's *The Evolution of Altruism and the Ordering of Love* (Washington, D.C.: Georgetown University Press, 1994).

3. Josiah Royce, *The Problem of Christianity* (New York: Macmillan, 1931), pp. 172–213.

4. Albert Camus, *The Fall,* trans. by Justin O'Brien (New York: Vintage Books, 1991 [original 1957]), p. 22.

5. Ibid., pp. 57, 59, 73, 91.

6. Ibid., p. 91.

7. Charles Dickens, *Bleak House* (New York: Oxford University Press, 1987 [original 1853]), pp. 36, 41, 537.

8. William H. McGuffey, "True and False Philanthropy," in *America's Voluntary Spirit: A Book of Readings,* ed. by Brian O'Connell, with a Foreword by John W. Gardner (New York: The Foundation Center, 1983 [original 1844]), pp. 59–61 (emphases in original).

9. Augustine, *On Christian Doctrine,* in *Augustine* (Great Books of the Western World), trans. by J. F. Shaw (Chicago: Encyclopedia Britannica, 1952 [original c. 427]), p. 632.

10. Henry Sidgwick, *The Methods of Ethics* (Indianapolis: Hackett Publishing, 1981 [original 1906]), p. 241.

11. Adam Smith, *The Theory of Moral Sentiments,* ed. by D. D. Raphael and A. L. Macfie (Indianapolis: Liberty Classics, 1982 [original 1759]), p. 216.

12. Ibid., p. 237.

13. Ibid., p. 237.

14. Marilyn Friedman, "The Social Self and the Partiality Debates," in *Feminist Ethics,* ed. by Claudia Card (Lawrence: University Press of Kansas, 1991), p. 163.

15. Lawrence C. Becker, "Impartiality and Ethical Theory," *Ethics: An International Journal of Social and Legal Philosophy (Symposium on Impartiality and Ethical Theory)* 101, no. 4 (July 1991), pp. 698, 699.

16. Joseph Butler, "Fifteen Sermons," in *British Moralists 1650–1800* ed. by D. D. Raphael (Oxford: Clarendon Press, 1969 [original 1726]), pp. 373, 374.

17. Lawrence C. Becker, *Reciprocity* (London: Routledge & Kegan Paul, 1986), p. 392.

18. For a brief summary of historical material, see Jeffrey Blustein, *Parents and Children: The Ethics of the Family* (New York: Oxford, 1982), section 1.

19. Thomas Aquinas, *Summa Theologiae,* trans. by D. J. Sullivan (Chicago: Encyclopedia Britannica Press, 1952), II–II, q. 26, a. 8.

20. Josiah Royce, *The Philosophy of Loyalty* (New York: Macmillan, 1908), p. 221.

21. John Rawls, *A Theory of Justice* (Cambridge, Mass.: Harvard University Press, 1971), p. 128.

22. Ibid., p. 463.

23. Friedrich A. Hayek, *The Constitution of Liberty* (Chicago: University of Chicago Press, 1960), p. 91.

24. Robert Nozick, *Anarchy, State, and Utopia* (New York: Basic Books, 1974), p. 167.

25. Michael Walzer, *Spheres of Justice: A Defense of Pluralism and Equality* (New York: Basic Books, 1983), pp. 230–231.

26. Adam Ferguson, *Principles of Moral and Political Science,* in *The Scottish Moralists: On Human Nature and Society,* ed. by Louis Schneider (Chicago: University of Chicago Press, 1967), p. 82.

27. Adam Smith, *The Theory of Moral Sentiments,* p. 219.

28. Ibid., p. 225.

29. Ibid., p. 237.

30. Alasdair MacIntyre, *After Virtue: A Study in Moral Theory* (Notre Dame: University of Notre Dame Press, 1981), p. 32.

31. Max Scheler, *Ressentiment,* ed. by Lewis A. Coser, trans. by William W. Holdheim (New York: Free Press, 1961 [original 1915]), pp. 96, 115, 116 (emphases in original).

32. Ernest Wallwork, *Psychoanalysis and Ethics* (New Haven: Yale University Press, 1991), p. 195 n. 4.

33. Ibid., p. 199.

34. Ibid., p. 200.

35. Ibid., p. 205.

36. Ibid., p. 207.

37. Don S. Browning, *Religious Thought and the Modern Psychologies* (Philadelphia: Fortress Press, 1987), pp. 153, 154.

38. Fyodor Dostoevsky, *The Brothers Karamazov,* trans. by Andrew H. MacAndrew (New York: Bantam Books, 1970 [original 1880]), pp. 65–67.

Selected
Bibliography

Full bibliographical data for all works cited in the text are supplied in the notes. The following bibliography lists only a selection of books that touch most deeply on the topic of this volume as a whole.

Bagot, Jean-Pierre. *How to Understand Marriage*. New York: Crossroad, 1987.

Bakan, David. *The Slaughter of the Innocents: A Study of the Battered Child Phenomenon*. Boston: Beacon Press, 1971.

Blustein, Jeffrey. *Parents and Children: The Ethics of the Family*. New York: Oxford University Press, 1982.

Browning, Don S. *Religious Thought and the Modern Psychologies*. Philadelphia. Fortress Press, 1987.

Brunner, Emil. *The Divine Imperative*. Trans. by Olive Wyon. Philadelphia: Westminster Press, 1937.

Cahill, Lisa Sowle. *Between the Sexes: Foundations for a Christian Ethics of Sexuality*. New York: Paulist Press, 1985.

Camus, Albert. *The Fall*. Trans. by Justin O'Brien. New York: Vintage Books, 1991 (original 1957).

Carr, Anne and Elisabeth Schussler Fiorenza, eds. *Motherhood: Experience, Institution, Theology*. Edinburgh: T & T Clark, 1989.

Coontz, Stephanie. *The Way We Never Were: American Families and the Nostalgia Trap*. New York: Basic Books, 1992.

Danagan, Alan. *The Theory of Morality*. Chicago: University of Chicago Press, 1977.

de Rougemont, Dennis. *Love in the Western World*. Trans. by Montgomery Belgion. New York: Harper & Row, 1956.

Dizard, Jan E. and Howard Gadlin. *The Minimal Family*. Amherst, Mass.: University of Massachusetts Press, 1990.

Epstein, Mark D. *Love's Compass: A Natural History of the Heart*. Reading, Mass.: Addison–Wesley, 1990.

Etzioni, Amitai. *The Spirit of Community: Rights, Responsibilities, and the Communitarian Agenda*. New York: Crown, 1993.

Gottlieb, Beatrice. *The Family in the Western World: From the Black Death to the Industrial Age*. New York: Oxford University Press, 1993.

Gustafson, James M. *Ethics from a Theocentric Perspective*, vol. 2, *Ethics and Theology*. Chicago: University of Chicago Press, 1984.

Hamburg, David A. *Today's Children: Creating a Future for a Generation in Crisis*. New York: Times Books, 1992.

Pollock, Linda A. *Forgotten Children: Parent-Child Relations from 1500 to 1900*. New York: Cambridge University Press, 1983.

Hauerwas, Stanley. *A Community of Character: Toward a Constructive Christian Social Ethics*. Notre Dame: University of Notre Dame Press, 1981.

Hazo, Robert. *The Idea of Love*. New York: Praeger, 1967.

Jewett, Paul K. *Man as Male and Female: A Study in Sexual Relationships from a Theological Point of View*. Grand Rapids, Mich.: William B. Eerdmans, 1975.

Kierkegaard, Soren. *The Concept of Anxiety: A Simple Psychologically Orienting Deliberation on the Dogmatic Issues of Hereditary Sin*. Trans. by T. Thomte. Princeton, N.J.: Princeton University Press, 1980 (1844 original).

McFague, Sallie. *Models of God: Theology for an Ecological Nuclear Age*. Philadelphia: Fortress Press, 1987.

McLanahan, Sara and Gary Sandefur. *Uncertain Childhood, Uncertain Future: Growing Up With a Single Parent*. Cambridge, Mass.: Harvard University Press, 1994.

Mehl, Roger. *Society and Love: Ethical Problems in the Family*. Trans. by James H. Farley. Philadelphia: Westminster Press, 1964.

Meilaender, Gilbert C. *The Limits of Love: Some Theological Explorations*. University Park, Pa.: The Pennsylvania State University Press, 1987.

Mercadante, Linda A. *Gender, Doctrine and God: The Shakers and Contemporary Theology*. Nashville: Abingdon Press, 1990.

Mollenkott, Virginia Ramey. *The Divine Feminine: The Biblical Imagery of God as Female*. New York: Crossroad, 1991.

Moynihan, Daniel Patrick. *Family and Nation*. San Diego: Harcourt Brace Jovanovich, 1986.

National Commission on Children. *Beyond Rhetoric: A New American Agenda for Children and Families*. Washington, D.C.: U.S. Government Printing Office, 1991.

National Research Council. *Losing Generations: Adolescents in High-Risk Settings*. Washington, D.C.: National Academy Press, 1993.

Nelson, James B. *Embodiment: An Approach to Sexuality and Christian Theology*. Minneapolis: Augsburg, 1979.

Nouwen, Henri J.M. *The Return of the Prodigal Son: A Meditation on Fathers, Brothers, and Sons*. New York: Doubleday, 1992.

Okin, Susan Moller. *Justice, Gender and the Family*. New York: Basic Books, 1989.

O'Neill, Onora and William Ruddick, eds. *Having Children: Philosophical and Legal Reflections on Parenthood*. New York: Oxford University Press, 1979.

Outka, Gene. *Agape: An Ethical Analysis*. New Haven, Conn.: Yale University Press, 1972.

Pagels, Elaine. *Adam, Eve, and the Serpent*. New York: Vintage Books, 1988.

Popenoe, David. *Disturbing the Nest: Family Change in Modern Societies*. Hawthorne, N.Y.: Aldine de Gruyter, 1988.

Pope, Stephen J. *The Evolution of Altruism and the Ordering of Love*. Washington, D.C.: Georgetown University Press, 1994.

Post, Stephen G. *A Theory of Agape: On the Meaning of Christian Love*. Lewisburg, Pa.: Bucknell University Press, 1990.

Ramsey, Paul. *Fabricated Man: The Ethics of Genetic Control*. New Haven, Conn.: Yale University Press, 1970.

Ruddick, Sara. *Maternal Thinking: Toward a Politics of Peace*. New York: Ballantine Books, 1989.

Sanders, E.P. *Jesus and Judaism*. Philadelphia: Fortress Press, 1985.

Singer, Irving. *The Nature of Love*. 3 Vols. Chicago: University of Chicago Press, 1987.

Soble, Alan. *The Structure of Love*. New Haven, Conn.: Yale University Press, 1990.

Taylor, Charles. *Sources of the Self: The Making of Modern Identity*. Cambridge, Mass.: Harvard University Press, 1989.

Thomas, Laurence. *Living Morally: A Psychology of Moral Character*. Philadelphia: Temple University Press, 1989.

Trebilcot, Joyce, ed. *Mothering: Essays in Feminist Theory*. Savage, Md.: Rowman & Littlefield, 1983.

Wadell, Paul J. *Friendship and the Moral Life*. Notre Dame, Ind.: University of Notre Dame Press, 1989.

Williams, Daniel Day. *The Spirit and the Forms of Love*. New York: Harper & Row, 1968.

Wyschogrod, Edith. *Saints and Postmodernism: Revisioning Moral Philosophy*. Chicago: University of Chicago Press, 1990.

Index

Agape. See Universal love

Aged. *See* Elderly persons

Ageism, 87

Allen, Jeffner, 59

Allen, Joseph L., 67

Analogical-familial theology, 25, 75–79; and development of moral awareness, 77

Aquinas, Saint Thomas. *See* Thomas Aquinas, Saint

Aristotle: *Politics,* 138

Asceticism, 41

Atonement, 122–123

Augustine, Saint, 7; *The City of God,* 101; on special relations, 133

Barth, Karl, 78; on conditionality of love, 118–121; on teaching function of the elderly, 87–88

Becker, Lawrence C., 135; on special relations and justice, 137–138

Bellah, Robert, 57, 97–98

Beneficence, order of. *See* Order of love

Benson, John, 59–60

Bergson, Henri, 69

Betz, Hans Dieter, 22

Bleak House (Dickens), 132

Blustein, Jeffrey, 82

Bok, Sissela, 13

Bridget, Saint (of Sweden), 25

Bronte, D. Lydia, 80

Brown, Gabrielle: *The New Celibacy,* 39

Browning, Don S., 94; on order of beneficence, 144

Brunner, Emil, 22, 61

Buber, Martin, 124

Burnaby, John, 77; theology of parental love, 61–62, 72

Butler, Joseph, 134; on familial love, 136–137

Butler, Robert N., 87

Cadoux, Cecil John, 24

Cahill, Lisa Sowle, 28

Callahan, Daniel, 93

Camus, Albert, 12, 35, 129; *The Fall,* 131–132

Caregiving, 92–93; burden upon women, 58–59, 102, 106–107; competing obligations, 104–105; increased need for, 94–96; and public policy, 104–105, 107; and self-denial, 102–105. *See also* Stewardship

Catholicism. *See* Roman Catholicism

Child care, 56
Childress, James F., 85
Christianity: attitude toward the sick, 113; Covenant metaphor, 85; and familial love, 13; and filial love, 80, 101; importance of child, 73–74; interpretation of Fall, 44–45; love of self and other, 61, 93; and marriage, 21–22, 48; and parental love, 61–62; and universal love, 111–112
Christian love. *See* Universal love
Cicero, 138
Civilization and Its Discontents (Freud), 143
Clement of Alexandria, 44–45
Colin, Louis, 67
Conjugal love. *See* Married love
Coontz, Stephanie, 3–4, 55
Covenantal relations, 85–88

Danielou, Jean, 42
D'Arcy, Martin, 116–117
Darling, Rosalyn, 99, 104
Decalogue, 80, 88
D'Emilio, John, 38
de Rougemont, Denis, 27
Dickens, Charles, 132
Distributive justice theory, 137–139
Divine pathos, 62–63, 123–125
Divine right of kings, 58
Divorce, 18, 19, 27, 28
Donagan, Alan, 3
Dostoyevsky, Fyodor Mikhaylovich: *The Adolescent (or A Raw Youth)*, 84–85; *The Brothers Karamazov*, 145
Duby, Georges, 30
Dyadic theism, 17, 20–24, 79; feminist concerns, 24–26

Edwards, Jonathan, 64–65
Elderly persons: and other-regarding love, 85–87; teaching function, 87–88
Emmet, Dorothy, 75
English, Jane, 100
Enlightenment, 145
Epstein, Daniel Mark, 71; on filial love, 72
Equalitarianism, 24–25
Essay on Man (Pope), 12–13, 31
Ethics: chief task of, 146; development of, 77; and familial love, 13, 101–102, 106, 142–143; feminist, 66; impersonal, 6–7, 113; and order of love, 7, 130, 141–142, 144; and parental love, 63–66; and partiality/impartiality debate, 134–137; personal, 6, 113; of sex, 41, 45–49; social, 6, 113; theological, 66–68, 76–77
Etzioni, Amitai, 51, 52; on divorce, 18; on solemnization of marriage, 19

Fall myth, 116; Irenaean interpretation, 153 n.28; sexual interpretation, 42–45
Familial love, 1–2, 12; extension to universal love, 59–60; social value, 138
Family: caregiving, 92–93, 94–96; decline of, 53–54, 55–57; ethics, 52, 106; new familialism, 2, 4, 55–56, 92, 95; nuclear, 2–4, 55–56, 92, 95; single-parent, 3, 56–57
Farley, Margaret A., 28, 59, 105
Fatherhood, 10, 54–55; patriarchal treatment of, 57–58

Featherstone, Helen, 98
Feminism: criticism of selfless
    mother love, 59; and dyadic
    theism, 24–26; and moral phi-
    losophy, 66; on patriarchal ma-
    nipulation of filial morality, 81;
    theology, 25
Ferguson, Adam, 141; on order
    of love, 134
Filial love, 10; absence of, 79–81;
    coerced, 58–59, 80–81; condi-
    tions for growth, 73; intergen-
    erational covenant, 87; and love
    for God, 88; morality of, 100–
    102; and parental love, 83–88;
    reciprocity, 71–74, 81–83, 88
Filmer, Sir Robert, 57–58
Fiorenza, Elisabeth S., 22
Firth, Rodrick, 135
Fleischman, Paul R., 37
Flew, R. Newton, 21
Freedman, Estelle B., 38
Freud, Sigmund, 36, 37; *Civiliza-
    tion and Its Discontents,* 143;
    *Group Psychology and the Analy-
    sis of the Ego,* 143; on order of
    love, 143–144
Friedman, Marilyn, 129; on im-
    partial observer, 135
Friendship, 125–126
Fromm, Erich, 78

Gaylin, Willard: on parental love,
    63–64; philosophy of sex,
    36–37
Gebara, Ivone, 58
Geisler, Norman A.: on parental
    love, 67
Gender equality: in the church,
    25; and family caregiving,
    93–94; in marriage, 27–28; in
    parenting, 54–55

Genesis, 61
Gleason, Edward S., 19
God: deep longing for, 122–123;
    images of, 25–26, 58, 79; love
    for, 78, 88, 122–125
Good Samaritan, 110, 111, 113,
    117–118
Greer, Germaine, 35
*Group Psychology and the
    Analysis of the Ego* (Freud),
    143
Gustafson, James M., 9, 31, 66,
    96, 99

Hall, Everett, 101
Hallett, Garth L., 93–94
Haring, Bernard, 101
Hartmann, Nicolai, 7
Hauerwas, Stanley, 8, 29, 59
Hayek, Friedrich A., 139
Hebrew Bible: divine pathos in,
    124–125; maternal images of
    God, 25; theological analogies
    to parent-child love, 78; use of
    word *father,* 62
Held, Virginia, 65
Henotheism, 127
Hermeneutics of cultural suspi-
    cion, 39–40
Heschel, Abraham, 63
Hume, David, 23

Impartiality/partiality. *See* Order
    of love
Impersonal ethics, 6–7, 113
Impersonal love. *See* Universal
    love
Irenaeus of Lyons, Saint, 44–45

James, William, 6
Janssens, Louis, 130
Jeremiah, 109

Jesus and Judaism (Sanders), 14–15
Jesus of Nazareth: centrality of familial, 13–15; on conditional love, 115; on divorce, 20; on importance of children, 73–74; parental metaphors of God, 62, 78
Judaism: Covenant metaphor, 85; and filial piety, 80; and marriage, 48; and parental love, 61
Julian of Norwich, 25, 124
Justice: distributive, 137–139; gender, 54–55; subsidiarity, 138–139

Kant, Immanuel, 9, 13, 32; on misuse of sex, 41, 47; theory of self, 142
Keller, Catherine, 8
Kierkegaard, Søren, 7, 40; *The Concept of Anxiety,* 43; on motivation of love, 114; neglect of family love, 143; sexual interpretation of the fall, 42–44, 152 n.18

Lasch, Christopher, 57
Lewis, C. S.: *The Abolition of Man,* 100; on sexual indulgence, 38–39
Libertarians, 139
Lifton, Robert Jay, 64
Locke, John, 57–58
Love: of bestowal, 114; conditionality, 111, 115–122, 127–128; defined, 4–6, 47; familial, 1–2, 7, 12, 59–60, 138; for God, 122–125; participatory, 125–126, 127; property-based, 114; spheres, 6–8; unconditionality, 11, 110–111,

112–118, 119, 127. *See also* Filial love; Parental love; Universal love
Luke, Saint, 71; intent of Christian love, 121
Luther, Martin, 22; on sex, 48

MacIntyre, Alisdair, 142
MacKinnon, Catherine A., 39
Marcel, Gabriel, 97
Marriage: ideal of, 18; in image of God *(in imagine Dei),* 20, 48–49; solemnization of, 19; theological meaning, 28–29; vows, 96
Married love, 17–20; in Christian thought, 29; as companionate love, 30; in image of God *(in imagine Dei),* 21–24, 29, 30, 31; and other special relations, 32; permanance, 26–29; and universal love, 31–33
Matthew, Saint, 109; intent of Christian love, 121
May, Larry, 54
May, Rollo, 38
May, William F., 76, 86–87
McFague, Sallie: image of God as mother-father, 58; importance of parental love, 52, 53
McGuffey, William H., 132–133
Medical technology, 95
Mehl, Roger, 31
Meilaender, Gilbert C., 8, 93; on sexual ethics, 45–46
Mekilta de-Rabbi Ishmael, 80–81
Mercadante, Linda A., 26
Metanoiai, 69
Mollenkott, Virginia Ramey, 25
Moody, Harry R., 91
Morality. *See* Ethics
Moses, 20

Moses Maimonides, 113
Motherhood, 59
Mother Teresa, 113

National Commission on Children, 3, 53
National Council of Churches, 25
Natural theology, 23; of parental love, 61
Nelson, James B., 40; *Embodiment*, 45 46
New Testament: *agape* in, 125; on filial love, 101; *philia* in, 125; theological analogies to parent-child love, 78
Newton, Isaac, 23
Niebuhr, H. Richard, 127
Niebuhr, Reinhold, 2, 51; on sexual character of sin, 42
Noddings, Nel, 73
Nouwen, Henri J., 74–75
Nozick, Robert, 139
Nuclear family, 55–56; caregiving crisis, 92, 95; importance, 4
Nygren, Anders, 2; on deep longing for God, 122; neglect of family love, 143; on unconditionality of love, 115–117, 119

Okin, Susan Moller, 9, 17, 91; on gendered marriage, 27; on sharing of caregiving, 93
Oppenheimer, Helen, 121–122; on God's love, 123–124
Order of love *(ordo caritatis)*, 1, 7, 129–130; in ethical theory, 134–137, 141–142
Original sin. *See* Fall myth
Outka, Gene, 94; interpretation of Barth, 118–121; theory of *agape*, 120

Pagels, Elaine H., 25, 44–45
Parental love, 33; as altruistic emotion, 60; criticisms of, 52, 57–60; effects of absence, 73, 79; ethical theory of, 18, 63–66; expansion into universal love, 63, 68–70; failures of, 79–80; in the image of God (*in imagine Dei*), 60–63; and impaired children, 98–99; in Judeo Christian thought, 58, 60–63, 67–68
Parenting deficit, 2–3, 53, 57; relation to economic decline, 55
Parrinder, Geoffrey, 20
Partiality/impartiality. *See* Order of love
Participatory love, 125–126, 127
Patriarcha (Filmer), 57–58
Patriarchism, 57–58, 62
Paul, Saint, 11, 22, 61; marriage as hindrance to evangelical activity, 24
Personal ethics, 6, 113
Philanthropia, 112–113
Philia, 125
Phillips, Dewi Z., 111
Plato, 138, 140
Pope, Alexander, 12–13, 31
Pope, Stephen J., 7; on *ordo caritatis*, 130
Popenoe, David, 2, 55, 56, 57
Prescott, James, 22–23
Prodigal son, 74–75, 116, 120
Psychoanalysis and Ethics (Wallwork), 143
Public policy: myth of family self-reliance, 104; toward family caretakers, 96, 104–105, 107–108
Purvis, Sally B., 7, 64

173

Rad, Gerhard von, 48
Ramsey, Paul, 61
Rauschenbusch, Walter, 32
Rawls, John, 139
Reciprocity: of love, 71–74,
    81–83, 88
Reed, Barbara E., 24–25
Religious love. *See* Universal
    love
Rembrandt, 74–75
Repentance, 122–123
Return of the Prodigal Son, The
    (Rembrandt), 74–75
Rist, John M., 115–116, 117,
    119, 122
Roman Catholicism: analogical
    theology, 78; *Familiaris Con-
    sortio* ("On the Family"), 68;
    and order of love, 130, 162
    n.2; and parental love, 58, 61,
    67–68; subsidiarity, 68,
    138–139
Romanticism, 29–31
Rousseau, Jean-Jacques, 54
Royce, Josiah, 130, 138
Ruddick, Sara, 66

Sanders, E. P., 14–15
Sanders, Jack T., 120–121
Sapp, Stephen, 85–86
Sartre, Jean-Paul, 97
Scheler, Max, 142–143
Scottish Enlightenment, 141
Secular modernity, 87–88
Self: philosophy of, 145; theories
    of, 142
Self-denial, 5, 102–105; limits on,
    10–11; and love, 94–96
Sex, 18; Christian view of, 40,
    42; ethics of, 41, 45–49; and
    love, 47; misuse of, 41, 43–44,
    47; in modern secular culture,

35–38; reflection of human
    disorder, 40–42; restraint from,
    44; as sinful, 42–45; substitu-
    tion for spirituality, 37
Shakers, 26
Sidgwick, Henry, 100; on order
    of love, 134
Simmons, Leo W., 86
Sin, 42–45
Single-parent families, 3, 56–57
Slote, Michael A., 58, 81
Smith, Adam: on order of love,
    134, 141–142; *Theory of Moral
    Sentiments,* 141
Social ethics, 6, 113
Sommers, Christina Hoff, 102
Special relations. *See* Familial
    love; Filial love; Parental
    love
Stendahl (Beyle, Marie-Henri),
    30
Stewardship: conjugal, 96–98;
    as a creative vocation, 99;
    ethic of, 95; obligations to self,
    103
Storge. See Parental love
Strategic conditionality, 111,
    115–118, 127–128
Strikwerda, Robert, 54
Subsidiarity, 138–139
Swinburne, Richard, 122–123

Temple, William, 17
Thecla, 44
Theological ethics, 76–77; non-
    feminist, 66–68. *See also*
    Analogical-familial theology
Thomas Aquinas, Saint: on order
    of love, 133, 143; *Summa The-
    ologiae,* 101, 133, 143
Tillich, Paul, 69
Tradition, loss of, 87–88

Trible, Phyllis, 25
"True and False Philanthropy"
(McGuffey), 132–133
Turner, Mark, 76
Turner, Philip, 19–20

Unconditional love, 11, 110–111,
112–118, 127
Universal love, 7, 12; as filial
love, 146; and friendship, 126;
and married love, 31–33; missionary intent, 118; in New
Testament, 125; as outgrowth
of filial love for God, 78; and
parental love, 68–70; strategic
conditionality, 111, 115–118,
127–128; unconditionality,
11, 110–111, 112–118, 119,
129
Utilitarianism, 7

Wacker, Marie-Theres, 62
Wadell, Paul J., 8, 125–126
Wallwork, Ernest, 143
Walzer, Michael, 139–141
Wayland, Francis, 27
Whitehead, Barbara Dafoe, 53
Williams, Bernard, 7
Williams, Daniel Day, 33, 60–61,
78; ethic of sex, 46–47
Women: as caregivers, 58–59,
102, 106–7; oppression of, 26;
and selflessness, 103
Wyschogrod, Edith, 6, 111–112

About the Author

STEPHEN G. POST received his Ph.D. from the University of Chicago Divinity School. Currently an associate professor at Case Western Reserve University, he has appointments in the Center for Biomedical Ethics, the Department of Religion, and the Department of Philosophy. He is a fellow of the Hastings Center and a Senior Research Fellow of the Kennedy Institute of Ethics at Georgetown University. His articles on love and ethics have appeared in many publications. *Inquiries in Bioethics* and *A Theory of Agape: On the Meaning of Christian Love* are his most recent books.

DATE DUE

Gardner-Webb Library
P.O. 836
Boiling Springs, NC 28017

DEMCO